THE BLOOD AND THE SPIRIT

OUR PRECIOUS SOURCE OF LIFE

ANDREW MURRAY

WHITAKER
HOUSE

Publisher's note:
This new edition from Whitaker House has been slightly abridged and updated for the modern reader. Words, expressions, and sentence structure have been revised for clarity and readability.

All Scripture quotations are taken from the King James Version of the Holy Bible.

The Blood and the Spirit

(formerly titled *The Blood of the Cross*)

ISBN: 978-1-64123-023-0
eBook ISBN: 978-1-64123-028-5
Printed in the United States of America
© 1981 by Whitaker House

Whitaker House
1030 Hunt Valley Circle
New Kensington, PA 15068
www.whitakerhouse.com

2 3 4 5 6 7 8 9 10 11 **W** 25 24 23 22 21 20 19 18

CONTENTS

ABOUT THE AUTHOR

Andrew Murray (1828–1917) was an amazingly prolific Christian author. He lived and ministered as both a pastor and a writer from the towns and villages of South Africa. All of his publications were originally written in Dutch and then translated into English. As his popularity grew, Murray's books found their way into more than twelve foreign languages in his lifetime alone.

Andrew Murray's earliest writings were primarily written for the edification of the believer—building them up in faith, love and prayer. They include books such as *Abide in Christ*, *Like Christ*, and *With Christ in the School of Prayer*. Later writings leaned more heavily upon the sanctification of the believer with such works as *Be Perfect*. Finally, in his last days, Murray addressed the issue of the church and its lack of power in the earth. He emphasized the need for a constant and vital relationship with Jesus Christ and for consistent, fervent prayer.

Murray was an alert and intense man, continuing on with his writings until his death at age eighty-nine. His burning desire to transpose all that lay on his heart and spirit to paper was revealed in the presence of several manuscripts in various stages of completion at the time of his death.

Andrew Murray has greatly blessed the Christian world with the richness of his spiritual wisdom and his ability to see and answer the needs of God's people.

PREFACE

In Andrew Murray's preface to the original edition, he gives his heartfelt reasons for sharing these messages which were such a great blessing to him.

He published them, he says, "because I am deeply convinced that we Christians can never know too much about the truths the blood proclaims. There can be no freedom of approach to God, nor fellowship with Him, apart from a truly vital and powerful experience of the blood of Christ. Its power is a hidden, spiritual, divine reality, and therefore can be experienced only in a heart that is humbly and entirely submitted to the Spirit of God. And in the same proportion that we have an insight into the inner nature that inspired Christ to shed His blood, we shall understand what the power is which can produce that same nature in us."

And so may it be that this newest version of Andrew Murray's classic will enlarge our vision of what Christ's blood has done and is still doing for us today. The heart and essence of Andrew Murray's messages are here. We have simply translated outdated words and phrases into those more commonly used so that the revelation of Murray's inspiring work would flow more smoothly for the reader.

We pray that the power and simplicity of this message would burn into the hearts and spirits of each of us as we see again what the Man has accomplished by His blood and His Spirit.

—*The Publisher*

1

THE SPIRIT AND THE BLOOD

And there are three that bear witness in earth, the Spirit, and the
water, and the blood: and these three agree in one.
—1 John 5:8

Before considering the blood of Jesus Christ and the glorious results which it accomplishes in us, there is a difficulty which must be overcome. We do not always enjoy the blessings and power of Christ's blood because we do not clearly understand what those benefits are or how the blood accomplishes them. Or, even if we do understand in some measure, it is not possible for us to always experience the blood's power because we do not always actively cooperate with it. Such difficulties arise because we do not remember that God has provided that the blood, as a vital power, automatically and ceaselessly carries on its work within us. He has so inseparably bound together the Holy Spirit and the blood that we may rely on Him to make the power of the blood ceaselessly effective in us by the power of the Spirit. This is the thought expressed in the above Scripture verse used for the text of this chapter. The apostle had in the previous verses (1 John 4–5) spoken about faith in Jesus, and then he directs attention to the testimony on which that faith rests (verses 8–11). He mentions three witnesses:

The Water: This refers to an outward and human act commanded by God to be observed by those who, turning from their sins, presented themselves to Him in baptism.

The Blood: In this we see what God has done to bring about a real and living cleansing.

The Spirit: It is by the Spirit that the witness of both the others is confirmed.

In this chapter we shall confine our attention to the truth that the united witness of the Spirit and the blood is the foundation of our faith.

Let us notice the unbroken union of these Witnesses:

1. In the work of redemption
2. In our personal experience

1. THE UNION OF THE SPIRIT AND THE BLOOD IN THE WORK OF REDEMPTION

What first demands our attention here is that it is through the Spirit alone that the blood has its power. We read in Hebrews 9:14: *"How much more shall the blood of Christ, who through the eternal Spirit offered himself without spot to God, purge your conscience from dead works to serve the living God."* The blood possesses its power to cleanse and to make us fit to serve the living God by the eternal Spirit who was in our Lord when He shed His blood. This does not mean merely that the Holy Spirit was in the Lord Jesus and bestowed on His person and His blood a divine worth. It is much more than that—it indicates that the shedding of His blood was brought about by the eternal Spirit, and that the Spirit lived and worked in that blood. As a result, when the blood was shed it could not decay as a dead thing, but as a living reality it could be taken up to heaven, to exercise its divine power from thence.

It is expressly for this reason that the Spirit is here called *"the eternal Spirit."* *Eternal* is one of the words of Scripture that everyone thinks he understands, but there are few who realize what a deep and glorious meaning it has. It is supposed that eternal is something that always continues, something that has no end. This explanation is a merely negative one and tells us only what eternal is not, but it teaches us nothing about its nature and being. Everything that exists in time has a beginning and is subject to the law of increase and decrease, of becoming and decaying.

What is eternal has no beginning and knows no change or weakening because it has in itself a life that is independent of time. In what is eternal there is no past that has already disappeared and is lost, and there is no future not yet possessed. It is always a glorious and endless present.

Now, when Scripture speaks of *eternal* life, *eternal* redemption, and *eternal* joy, it means much more than to say merely they will have no end. By that word we are taught that he who has a share in eternal blessedness possesses something in which the power of an endless life is at work. It is something in which there can be no change, nor can it suffer any diminution. And, therefore we may always enjoy it in the fullness of its life—bestowing blessings.

The object of Scripture in using that word is to teach us that if our faith lays hold of what is eternal, it will manifest itself in us as a power superior to all the fluctuations of our mind or feelings, with a youth which never grows old, and with a freshness which does not for a moment wither.

From this Scripture we are taught something also about the blood of Jesus, "*Who through the eternal Spirit offered himself without spot to God*" (Hebrews 9:14). Not only had the act of shedding His blood an eternally availing worth, the blood itself has Spirit and life in it. The blood is made effective by the power of an eternal life. This is why the epistle to the Hebrews lays much emphasis on the work of Christ as being once for all and eternal. Notice the expression in Hebrews 7:17: He is "*a priest for ever after the order of Melchizedek.*" "*After the power of an endless life*" (verse 16). He has an "*unchangeable priesthood. Wherefore he is able also to save them to the uttermost that come unto God by him, seeing he ever liveth to make intercession for them*" (verses 24–25). He is "*the Son, who is consecrated for evermore*" (verse 28). Further on we read (Hebrews 9:12): "*By his own blood he entered in once into the holy place, having obtained eternal redemption for us*"; and in 10:14: "*By one offering he hath perfected forever them that are sanctified.*" It speaks also of "*the blood *of the everlasting covenant"* (Hebrews 13:20). By the eternal Spirit the blood has obtained an eternal, ever-availing, ever-fresh, independent, imperishable power of life.

But the correlative is also true. As the blood possesses its power through the Spirit, so the Spirit manifests His full power and works effectively among men only through the blood. We know that the outpouring of the blood was followed by the outpouring of the Spirit. And we know the reason for this. By sin, a middle wall of partition separated God and man. "The flesh" was the veil that made true union impossible. As long as sin was not atoned for, God, by His Spirit, could not take up a settled abode in the heart of man. Until the power of the flesh was broken and subdued, the Spirit could not manifest His authority. For this reason, there is no mention in the days of the Old Testament of an outpouring of the Spirit of God except as a prediction of what should be in the last days. Also our Lord Jesus was not in a position to bestow upon His disciples the Spirit with whom He had been baptized, even though He took them into the closest fellowship with Himself, though He greatly loved them and longed to bless them.

Our Lord had to die before He could baptize with the Holy Spirit. The blood is the life of man; the Spirit is the life of God. Man must sacrifice his sinful life, bear the penalty of his sin, and surrender himself entirely to God before God could dwell in him with His life. What man himself could not do, that the Lord Jesus, the Son of Man, did for him. He shed His blood; He gave His life in entire surrender to the will of God as a satisfaction of the penalty of sin. When that was accomplished, it was possible for Him to receive the Spirit from the Father that He might pour Him out. The outpouring of the blood rendered possible the outpouring of the Spirit.

This is declared in the Scriptures in such words as these: *"The Holy Ghost was not yet given; because that Jesus was not yet glorified"* (John 7:39). And again: *"He shewed me a pure river of water of life, clear as crystal, proceeding out of the throne of God and of the Lamb"* (Revelation 22:1). It was when the Lamb took possession of the throne with the Father that the Spirit could flow out as a river. In the preaching of John the Baptist these were, also, the two statements he made about Jesus: *"Behold the Lamb of God, which taketh away the sin of the world,"* (John 1:29), and this *is He who baptizeth with the Holy Ghost"* (verse 33).

It was necessary for our High Priest to enter into "the holiest" with His blood and, having come out again, to appear before the throne with that blood. Only then could He bestow the Spirit from the throne as the seal that His work in the holiest had wrought out a perfect reconciliation. The blood and the Spirit are inseparable, for only through the blood can the Spirit dwell in man.

In the execution of the work of redemption, also, the activities of the blood and the Spirit are inseparably connected. This is why we find in Scripture that what in one place is ascribed to the Spirit is in another place ascribed to the blood, and the work of sanctification is ascribed to both the blood and the Spirit. Life also is ascribed to both. Our Lord said: *"Who so eateth my flesh, and drinketh my blood, hath eternal life,"* adding afterwards, *"It is the spirit that quickeneth; the flesh profiteth nothing"* (John 6:54, 63). We find similar expressions in the epistle to the Ephesians. After having said, *"Ye…are made nigh by the blood of Christ"* (Ephesians 2:13), a little later Paul declares (verse 18) that *"We…have access by one Spirit unto the Father."* So also in the epistle to the Hebrews, the scorning of the blood and of the Spirit is treated as one act. We read of those who *"counted the blood of the covenant…an unholy thing, and have done despite unto the Spirit of grace"* (Hebrews 10:29).

We have noticed that *"the blood"* is a word chosen by God as a short way of expressing certain thoughts, powers, and characteristics that are, as it were, included in it. It is not always easy, either in preaching or in personal exercise of faith, to find a perfect expression of these thoughts, powers, and characteristics. But this is what the Holy Spirit undertakes as His work, especially where faith is exercised about the blood. He will explain, and make living, the full and glorious meaning of the word. By enlightening our understanding, He will make clear to us the great thoughts of God that are contained in the words "the blood." Even before the understanding can lay hold of them, He will make their power active in the soul. And where a heart desiring salvation is humbly and reverently seeking for the blessings they bring, He will bestow them. And He will not only send the power of the blood *to* the heart, but will so reveal it *in* the heart that the same inner nature which inspired Jesus in the shedding of His blood will be awakened in us, as it is written: *"They overcame…by the blood of the Lamb…and they loved not their lives unto the death"* (Revelation 12:11).

It is the great work of the Holy Spirit to glorify Jesus and to make Him glorious in human hearts, by bestowing the blessed experience of His redemption. And because the blood is the central point of redemption, the Holy Spirit will make the blood appear especially glorious *to* us and will glorify it *in* us. We can form some idea of the blood that was shed on earth in connection with the sin offering, but we have little conception of the blood that in "the holiest" on high speaks and works in the power of eternal life. The Holy Spirit, however, comes with His heavenly, life-giving power to enable us to appropriate that which is eternal and to make it a real, living, inward experience in us.

Faith in the atoning power of the blood and in the personality of the Holy Spirit are two truths that are both denied when the church turns aside to error, while both of them are held fast by the true church of God. Where the blood is honored, preached, and believed in as the power of full redemption, there the way is opened for the fullness of the Spirit's blessing. And, in proportion, as the Holy Spirit truly works in the hearts of man, He always leads them to glory in the blood of the Lamb. *"And I beheld, and, lo, in the midst of the throne…stood a Lamb as it had been slain, having…seven eyes which are the seven Spirits of God"*

(Revelation 5:6). The blood and the Spirit proceed together from the Lamb, and together they bear witness to Him alone.

2. THE UNION OF THE SPIRIT AND THE BLOOD IN OUR PERSONAL EXPERIENCE

We lay emphasis on this to show what rich comfort and blessing this truth contains for us. We must once again notice the two sides of this truth: the blood exercises its full power through the Spirit, and the Spirit manifests His full power through the blood.

The blood exercises its full power through the Spirit. We have here a glorious answer to the questions that at once arise in the minds of seekers after salvation. I have no doubt that by what has been written on the power of the blood of Jesus—about the rich, full blessing that is found in that blood—that questions have arisen such as:

"How is it that the blood does not produce more results in my life?"

"How can I experience its full power?"

"Is there any hope for a person so weak as I am, and one who understands so little, to expect that fullness of blessing?"

Listen to the answer, all you who heartily and sincerely long for it. The Holy Spirit dwells within you, and it is His office to glorify the Lamb and the blood of the Lamb. The Spirit and the blood bear witness together. The mistake we make is in thinking of the blood as if it alone bare witness. We think of the shedding of the blood as an event that occurred nineteen hundred years ago on which we are to look back and, by the exercise of faith, to represent it as present and real. But, as our faith is always weak, we feel that we cannot do this as it ought to be done. As a result of this mistaken idea, we have no powerful experience of what the blood can do.

This weakness of faith arises, in the case of honest hearts, from imperfect conceptions concerning the power of the blood. If I regard the blood, not as something that lies inactive and must be aroused to activity by my faith, but as an almighty, eternal power that is always active, then my faith becomes, for the first time, a true faith. Then I shall understand that my weakness cannot interfere with the power of the blood. I have simply to honor the blood by exalted ideas of its power to overcome every hindrance. The blood will manifest its power in me, because the eternal Spirit of God always works *with* it and *in* it.

Was it not through the eternal Spirit that, when Jesus died, His blood had power to conquer sin and death, so that Jesus was *"brought again from the dead…through the blood of the everlasting covenant"* (Hebrews 13:20)?

Was it not through the eternal Spirit that the blood penetrated the regions of holy light and life to heaven itself and bears there its peculiar relationship to God the Father and to Jesus the mediator?

Is it not through the eternal Spirit that the blood ever continues to manifest its power on the innumerable multitude which is being gathered together? Is it not the eternal Spirit who dwells in me as a child of God, on whom I may rely to make the blood of Jesus glorious in me also? Thank God, it is so. I have no need to fear. In the childlike heart, conscious of its weakness and wholly surrendered to the Lamb of God in order to experience the power of His blood, the Holy Spirit will do His work. We may confidently rely upon the Spirit to reveal in us the omnipotent effects of the blood. But there is another difficulty. Even once we recognize that the blood is omnipotent in its effects, we often limit the continuance of its activities to the period of our own active cooperation with it. You imagine that, so long as you can *think* about it, and your faith is actively engaged with it, the blood will manifest its power in you. But there is a very large part of your life during which you must be engaged with earthly business, and you do not believe that, during these hours, the blood can continue its active work quite undisturbed. And yet it is so. If you have the necessary faith, if you definitely commit yourself to the sanctifying power of the blood for those hours during which you cannot be thinking about it, then you can be sure that your soul may continue, undisturbed, under the blessed activities of the blood. That is the meaning, the comfort, of what we said about the word eternal and the eternal redemption that the blood has purchased.

Eternal is that in which "the power of an imperishable life" works ceaselessly every moment. Through the eternal Spirit, the precious blood possesses this ceaselessly effective power of eternal life. The soul may, with even greater confidence, entrust itself to Him for every hour of business engagements, or of special rush and bustle, for the activity of the blood will continue without hindrance. Just as a fountain that is supplied by or from an abundant store of water streams out day and night with a cleansing and refreshing flow, so the blessed streams of this fountain of life will flow over and through the soul that dares to expect it from his Lord. And just as the Holy Spirit is the life-power of these omnipotent and ever-flowing streams of the blessed power of the blood, so it is He also who prepares us and makes it possible for us to recognize and receive these streams by faith. Spiritual things must be spiritually discerned. Our human thought cannot apprehend the mysteries of "the holiest" in heaven. This is especially true concerning the unspeakable glory of the holy blood in heaven. Let us with deep reverence entrust ourselves to the teaching of the Spirit, waiting on Him in holy stillness and awe that He may witness with, and of, the blood.

At Easter time we remember the passion and resurrection of our Lord and look forward to Pentecost[1] and the days of prayer during which we wait on the Lord, that we may be filled by His Spirit.

Each year we are thus reminded that it is the will of Him who baptizes with the Holy Spirit that His disciples should be filled with the

---

1. *Note from the translator:* The Dutch Reformed Church in South Africa for many years observed the ten days between Ascension and Pentecost as days of continuous and united prayer. It is impossible to tell how great and abiding has been the blessing of God on these gatherings.

Spirit. *"Full of the Holy Ghost"* (Acts 11:24) is not set forth in Scripture as the privilege of a particular time, or of a certain people, but is plainly represented as the privilege of every believer who surrenders himself to live wholly for, and in fellowship with, Jesus. Pentecost is not just a remembrance of something that once happened and then passed away, but it is the celebration of the opening of a fountain that ever flows. It is the promise of that which is always right, and the characteristic of those who belong to the Lord. We ought to be, and we must be, filled with the Holy Spirit.

The lesson that the Word of God has taught us shows the preparation necessary for the baptism of the Spirit. For the first disciples, as well as for the Lord Jesus, the path to Pentecost ran by Golgotha. The outpouring of the Spirit is inseparably bound up with the previous outpouring of the blood. With us also it is a new and deeper experience of what the blood can accomplish that will lead us to the full blessing of Pentecost.

Oh, the blessedness of a heart by blood made clean and filled with the Spirit. Full of joy and full of love, full of faith and full of praise, full of zeal and full of power—for the work of the Lord. By the blood and the Spirit of the Lamb, that heart is a temple where God dwells on His throne of grace, where God Himself is the light, where God's will is the only law, where the glory of God is all in all. Oh, ye children of God, come and let the precious blood prepare you for being filled with His Spirit, so that the Lamb that was slain for you may have the reward of His labor—labor marked by blood. And He and you together may be satisfied in His love.

2

THE BLOOD OF THE CROSS

[God] *having made peace through the blood of his cross, by him to*
reconcile all things unto himself; by him, whether they be things in
earth, or things in heaven.
—Colossians 1:20

The apostle uses here an expression of deep significance: *"the blood of his cross."* We know how greatly he valued the expression *"the cross of Christ"* (1 Corinthians 1:17). It expressed, in a brief phrase, the entire power and blessing of the death of our Lord for our redemption, the subject of his preaching, and the hope and glory of his life. By the expression used here, Paul shows how, on the one side, the blood possesses its value from the cross on which it was shed, and on the other side that it is through the blood that the cross reveals its effect and power. Thus, the cross and the blood throw reflected light on one another. In our inquiry concerning the power of the blood, we shall find it of great importance to consider what this expression has to teach us, what is meant by the blood as "the blood of the cross." It will enable us to view from a new standpoint the truths that we have already discovered in that phrase *"the blood."*

Let us fix our attention on the following points:

1. The Nature of the Cross

2. The Power of the Cross

3. The Love of the Cross

1. THE NATURE OF THE CROSS

We are so accustomed, in speaking about the cross of Christ, to think only of the work that was done there for us that we take too little notice of the source from which that work derives its value—the inner nature of our Lord of which the cross was only the outward expression. Scripture does not place in the foreground, as most important, the weighty and bitter sufferings of the Lord that are often emphasized for the purpose of awakening religious feelings. But the inner nature of the Lord, which led Him to the cross and inspired Him while on it—this Scripture does emphasize. Neither does Scripture direct attention only to the work that the Lord accomplished for us on the cross. It directs special attention to the work that the cross accomplished in Him, and that through Him must yet be accomplished in us also.

The Lord Jesus, who came to deliver man from sin as a whole, had to deal with the *power* of sin as well as with its *guilt*; first the one, and then the other. For although we separate these two things for the sake of making truth clear, sin is ever a unity. Therefore, we need to understand not only that our Lord, by His atonement on the cross, removed the guilt of sin, but that this was made possible by the victory He had first won over the power of sin. It is the glory of the cross that it was the divine means by which both these objects were accomplished. The Lord Jesus had to bring to naught the power of sin. He could do this only in His own person. Therefore, he came in the closest possible likeness of sinful flesh, in the weakness of flesh, with the fullest capacity to be tempted as we are. From His baptism with the Holy Spirit and the temptation of Satan that followed, up to the fearful soul agony in Gethsemane and the offering of Himself on the cross—His life was a ceaseless strife against self-will and self-honor, against the temptation of trying to reach His goal—the setting up of His kingdom—by fleshly or worldly means. Every day He had to take up and carry His cross. That is, to lose His own life and will by going out of Himself and doing and speaking nothing except what he had seen or heard from the Father.

That which took place in the temptation in the wilderness and in the agony of Gethsemane—at the beginning and end of His public ministry—is only a peculiarly clear manifestation of the inner nature that characterized His whole life. He was tempted to the sin of self-assertion, but He overcame the temptation to satisfy lawful desires—from the first temptation, to obtain bread to satisfy His hunger, till the last, that He might not have to drink the bitter cup of death—that He might be subject to the will of the Father.

So He offered up Himself and His life; He denied Himself and took up His cross; He learned obedience and became perfect. In His own person He gained a complete victory over the power of sin, till He was able to testify that the evil one, *"the prince of this world cometh, and hath nothing in me"* (John 14:30). His death on the cross was the last and most glorious achievement in His personal victory over the power of sin, from this the atoning death of the cross derived its value. For a reconciliation was necessary if guilt was to be removed. No one can contend with sin without at the same time coming into conflict with the wrath of God. These two cannot be separated from one another. The Lord Jesus desired to deliver man from his sin. He could not do this except by suffering death as mediator, and in that death suffering the curse of God's wrath against sin and bearing it away. But His supreme power to remove guilt and the curse did not lie merely in the fact that He endured so much pain and suffering of death, but that he endured it all *in willing obedience to the Father* for the maintenance and glorification of His righteousness. It was this inner nature of self-sacrifice, the bearing of the cross willingly, which bestowed on the cross its power.

So the Scripture says he *"became obedient unto death, even the death of the cross. Wherefore God also hath highly exalted him, and given him a name which is above every name"* (Philippians 2:8–9). And again: *"Yet learned he obedience by the things which he suffered; and being made perfect, he became the author of eternal salvation unto all them that obey him"* (Hebrews 5:8-9). It is because Jesus broke down and conquered the power of sin first in His personal life that He can remove from us the guilt of sin, and thus deliver us from both its power and guilt. The cross is the divine sign proclaiming to us that the way, the only way, to the life of God is through the yielding up in sacrifice of the self-life. Now, this spirit of obedience, this sacrifice of self, which bestowed on the cross its infinite value, bestowed that value also on the blood of the cross. Here again, God reveals to us the secret of the power of that blood. That blood is the proof of obedience unto death by the beloved Son. It is proof of that inner nature that chose to offer it (the blood), to shed it, and to lose His own life rather than commit the sin of pleasing Himself. It is the sacrifice of everything, even life itself, to glorify the Father. The life that dwelt in that blood—the heart from which it flowed—glowing with love and devotion to God and His will was one of entire obedience and consecration to Him.

And now, what do you think? If that blood, living and powerful through the Holy Spirit, comes into contact with our hearts, and if we rightly understand what the blood of the cross means, is it possible that that blood should not impart its holy nature to us? But as the blood could not have been shed apart from the sacrifice of "self" on the cross, so it cannot be received or enjoyed apart from a similar sacrifice of self. That blood will bring to us a self-sacrificing nature. And in our work there will be a conformity to, and an imitation of, the crucified One, making self-sacrifice the highest and most blessed law of our lives. The blood is a living, spiritual, heavenly power. It will cause the soul that is entirely surrendered to it to see and know by experience that there is no entrance into the full life of God, except by the self-sacrifice of the cross.

2. THE POWER OF THE CROSS

As we pay attention to this, we shall have a deeper insight into the meaning of the cross and *"the blood of his cross"* (Colossians 1:20). The apostle Paul speaks of the word of the cross as *"the power of God"* (Romans 1:16).

We want to know what the cross as the power of God can accomplish. We have seen the twofold relationship our Lord has towards sin. First, He must in Himself, as man, subdue its *power*; then He can destroy its effects before God as *guilt*. The one was a process carried on through His whole life; the other took place in the hour of His passion. Now that He has completed His work, we may receive both blessings at the same time. Sin is a unity, so is redemption. We receive in an equal share both deliverance from the power of sin and acquittal from its guilt at the same time. As far as consciousness is concerned, however, acquittal from guilt comes earlier than a clear sense of the forgiveness of sins. It cannot be otherwise. He (our Lord) had first to obtain the blotting out of guilt through His victory over sin, and then he entered heaven. The blessing comes to us in the reverse order. Redemption descends upon us as a gift from above, and therefore restoration of a right relationship to God comes first, and we receive deliverance from guilt. Along with that, and flowing from it, comes deliverance from the power of sin.

This twofold deliverance we owe to the power of the cross. Paul speaks of the first, deliverance from guilt, in the words of our text. He says that God has become reconciled, *"having made peace by the blood of his cross"* (Colossians 1:20), with a view to reconciling all things to Himself.

Sin had brought about a change in God, not in His nature, but in His relationship towards us. He had to turn away from us in wrath. Peace has been made through the cross of Christ. By reconciliation for sin, God has reconciled us with and united us to Himself. The power of the cross in heaven has been manifested in the entire removal of everything that could bring about a separation from God or awaken His wrath. Now, in Christ we are granted the utmost freedom of entrance *to* and the most intimate relationship *with* God. Peace has been made and proclaimed; peace reigns in heaven. We are perfectly reconciled to God and have been received again into His friendship.

But the powerful effect of the cross in the blotting out of guilt and our renewed union with God is, as we have seen, inseparable from that other effect—the breaking down of the authority of sin over man by the sacrifice of self. Therefore, Scripture teaches us that the cross not only works out a desire to make such a sacrifice, but it really bestows the power to do so and completes the work. This appears with wonderful clearness in the epistle to the Galatians. In one place the cross is spoken of as the reconciliation for guilt, *"Christ hath redeemed us from the curse of the law, being made a curse for us: for it is written, Cursed is every one that hangeth on a tree"* (Galatians 3:13). But there are three other places where the cross is even more plainly spoken of as the victory over the power of sin; as the power to put to death the "I" of the self-life, of the flesh, and of the world. *"I am crucified with Christ: nevertheless I live; yet not I, but Christ liveth in me"* (Galatians 2:20). *"And they that are Christ's have crucified the flesh with the affections and lusts"* (Galatians 5:24). *"But God forbid that I should glory, save in the cross of our Lord Jesus Christ, by whom the world is crucified unto me, and I unto the world"* (Galatians 6:14). In these passages, our union with Christ, the crucified One, and the conformity to Him resulting from that union are represented as the result of the power exercised on us by the cross.

To understand this we must remember that when Jesus chose the cross, took it up, carried it, and finally died on it, He did this as the second Adam, as the Head and Surety of His people. What He did had and retains power for them and exercises that power in those who understand and believe this. The life that He bestows on them is a life in which the cross is the most outstanding characteristic. Our Lord carried His cross all through His entire life as a mediator. By dying on that cross as a mediator, He obtained the life of glory. As the believer is united to Him and receives his life, he receives a life that, through the cross, has overthrown the power of sin, and he can henceforth say, "I am crucified with Christ. I know that my old man is crucified with Christ. I am dead to sin. I have crucified the flesh. I am crucified to the world." (See Romans 6:6, 11.) All these expressions from God's Word refer to something that occurred in a time now past. The Spirit and life of Jesus bestow on believers their share in the victory over sin that was achieved on the cross.

And now, in the power of this participation and fellowship, they live as Jesus lived. They live always as those crucified to themselves, as those who know that their "old man" and "flesh" are crucified so as to be put to death. In the power of this fellowship, they live as Jesus lived. They have the power in all things and all times to choose the cross in spite of the "old man" and the world, to choose the cross and to let it do its work.

The law of life for Jesus was the surrender of His own will to that of the Father by giving up that life to death. Therefore He entered upon the heavenly life of redemption through the cross to the throne. So, as surely as there is a kingdom of sin, under the authority of which we were brought by our connection with the first Adam, so surely has there been set up a new kingdom of grace, in Christ Jesus, under the powerful influence of which we are brought by faith. The marvelous power by which Jesus subdued sin on the cross lives and works in us, and not only calls us to life as He lived, but enables us to do so, to adopt the cross as the motto and law of our lives.

Believer, that blood with which you have been sprinkled, under which you live daily, is the blood of the cross. It obtains its power from the fact that it was the complete sacrifice of a life to God. The blood and the cross are inseparably united. The blood comes from the cross; it bears witness to the cross; it leads to the cross. The power of the cross is in that blood. Every touch of the blood should inspire you with a fresh ability to take the cross as the law of your life. "*Not my will, but thine be done*" (Luke 22:42), may now, in that power, become a song of daily consecration. What the cross teaches you that it bestows upon you; what it imposes upon you that it makes possible for you. Let the everlasting sprinkling of the blood of the cross be your choice. Then, through that blood, the nature as well as the power of the cross will be seen in you.

3. THE LOVE OF THE CROSS

We must now fix our attention on this, if we are to learn the full glory of the blood of the cross.

We have spoken of the inner nature of which the cross is the expression and of the powerful influence that inner nature exercises in and through us if we allow the blood of the cross to have its full power over us. The fear, however, often arises in the mind of the Christian that it is too much of a burden always to preserve and manifest that inner quality. And even the assurance that the cross is the power of God, which produces that quality, does not entirely remove the fear. This is because the exercise of that power depends to some extent on our surrender and faith, and these are far from being what they ought to be. Can we find in the cross a deliverance from this infirmity, the healing of this disease? Cannot the blood of the cross make us partakers always, without ceasing, not only of the blotting out of guilt, but also of victory over the power of sin?

It can. Draw near to hear once more what the cross proclaims to you. It is only when we understand aright and receive into our hearts the love of which the cross speaks that we can experience its full power and blessing. Paul indeed bears witness to this: *"I am crucified with Christ: nevertheless I live; yet not I, but Christ liveth in me: and the life which I now live in the flesh I live by the faith of the Son of God, who loved me, and gave Himself for me"* (Galatians 2:20).

Faith in the love of Him who *"gave Himself for me"* on the cross enables me to live as one who has been crucified with Him.

The cross is the revelation of love. He saw that there was no other way by which His love could redeem those whom He so loved, except by shedding His blood for them on the cross. It is because of this that He would not allow Himself to be turned aside by the terror of the cross, not even when it caused His soul to tremble and shudder. The cross tells us that He loved us so truly that His love surmounted every difficulty—the curse of sin and the hostility of man—that His love has conquered and has won us for Himself. The cross is the triumphant symbol of eternal love. By the cross love is seated on the throne, so that from the place of omnipotence it can now do for the beloved ones all that they desire.

What a new and glorious light is thus shed on the demand the cross makes on me, on what it offers to do for me, on the meaning and glory and life of the cross to which I have been called by the Word. My flesh is so disposed to go astray that even the promise of the Spirit and the power of heaven seem insufficient to bestow on me the courage I need. But lo! Here is something that is better still than the promise of power. The cross points out to me the living Jesus in His eternal, all-conquering love. Out of love to us He gave Himself up to the cross, to redeem a people for Himself. In this love, He accepts everyone who comes to Him in the fellowship of His cross, to bestow upon them all the blessings that He had obtained on that cross. And now He receives us in the power of His eternal love, which ceases not for one moment to work out in us what He obtained for us on the cross.

I see it! What we need is a right view of Jesus Himself, and of His all-conquering, eternal love. The blood is the earthly token of the heavenly glory of that love; the blood points to that love. What we need is to behold Jesus Himself in the light of the cross. All the love manifested by the cross is the measure of the love He bears to us today. The love that was not terrified by any power or opposition of sin will now conquer everything in us that would be a hindrance. The love which triumphed on the accursed tree is strong enough to obtain and maintain a complete victory over us. The love manifested by *"a Lamb as it had been slain"* (Revelation 5:6) in the midst of the throne, bearing always the marks of the cross, lives solely to bestow on us the inner nature and power and the blessing of that cross. To know Jesus in His love, to live in that love, and to have the heart filled with that love is the greatest blessing that the cross can bring to us. It is the way to the enjoyment of all the blessings of the cross. Glorious cross! Glorious cross that brings to us and makes known to us the eternal love. The blood is the fruit and power of the cross; the blood is the gift and bestowal of that love. In what a full enjoyment of love those may now live who have been brought into such wonderful contact with the blood, who live every moment under its cleansing. How wondrously that blood unites us to Jesus and His love.

Beloved Christian, whose hope is in the blood of the cross, give yourself up to experience its full blessing. Each drop of that blood points to the surrender and death of self-will and of the "I" life, as the way to God and life in Him. Each drop of that blood assures you of the power obtained by Jesus on the cross to maintain that inner nature and that crucified life, in you. Each drop of that blood brings Jesus and His eternal love to you, to work out all the blessing of the cross in you, and to keep you in that love.

May each thought of the cross and the blood bring you nearer to your Savior and into a deeper union with Him, to whom they point.

3

THE ALTAR SANCTIFIED
BY THE BLOOD

Seven days thou shalt make an atonement for the altar,
and sanctify it; and it shall be an altar most holy: whatsoever toucheth
the altar shall be holy.
—Exodus 29:37

Of all the articles in the furnishing of the tabernacle, the altar was in many respects the most important. The golden mercy seat on which God manifested His visible glory in the Most Holy place within the veil was more glorious. It was, however, hidden from the eyes of Israel, being the representation of the hidden presence of God in heaven. Only once each year was Israel's active faith intentionally fixed on it. But at the altar, on the other hand, God's priests were continually engaged every day. The altar might be likened to a door of entrance to all the service of God in the Holy Place. Before there was either a temple or tabernacle, an altar served as a place for the worship of God, as in the case of Noah and the patriarchs. Man may worship God without a temple, if he has an altar. But he may not worship God without an altar—even if he has a temple. Before God spoke to Moses at Sinai about a tabernacle where He might dwell among the people, He had already spoken to him about sacrificial worship. The service of the altar was the beginning, the center, indeed the heart of the service of the tabernacle and temple.

Why was that? What was the altar? And why did it occupy such an important position? The Hebrew word for altar gives the answer. It means, specifically, the place of putting to death, of killing. Even the place of incense—where there was no slain victim—bore the name of altar because gifts offered in sacrifice to God were laid upon it. The chief thought is this: that man's service for God consists in the sacrifice and consecration of himself and all he has to God. To this end there had to be a separated place, ordered and sanctified by God Himself. Because the altar was ordered and sanctified by Him, it sanctifies and makes the gift that is laid upon it acceptable. The one with the offering brings to it not only the sacrifice that is to atone for his sins, but also the thank-offering that follows reconciliation. This is the expression of his love and thankfulness, of his desire for closer fellowship with God and for the full enjoyment of His favor. The altar is the place of sacrifice, of consecration, and also of fellowship with God.

The altar of the Old Testament must have an anti-type in the New Testament; something that in spiritual worship is the perfect reality of which the Old Testament altar was only the shadow. *"We have an altar,"* says the Holy Spirit in Hebrews 13:10. In the eternal activities of heaven there is also an altar. *"And another angel came and stood at the altar, having a golden censer....And the angel took the censer, and filled it with fire of the altar"* (Revelation 8:3, 5). That altar in the New Testament, no less than that of the Old Testament, was a place for putting to death, a place of sacrifice. It is not difficult to tell where that place is that is spoken of in the New Testament. It is the altar where, once for all, the Lamb of God was sacrificed as the great sin-offering, where also each believer must present himself with all that he has as a thanks offering to God. That altar is the cross.

In our text we learn that the altar itself had to be sanctified by blood if it was to possess the power of sanctifying whatever touched it. Our text tells us of:

1. The Altar Sanctified by Blood

2. The Offering Sanctified by the Altar

May the Spirit of God open our eyes to see the full power of the blood of the cross. May we see the sanctification of the cross as the place of our death, and the place where we also may be consecrated to God.

1. THE ALTAR SANCTIFIED BY BLOOD

It is in the midst of the instructions concerning the consecration of Aaron as High Priest (his sons being consecrated with him as priests) that the words of the text appear. A priest must have an altar. But just as the priest himself had to be sanctified by blood, so was it also with the altar. God commanded that a sin-offering should be prepared to cleanse the altar and to make atonement for it.

For seven days Moses had to carry on this work of making atonement for the altar.

We read: "*And Moses took the blood* [of the sin offering], *and put it upon the horns of the altar round about with his finger, and purified the altar, and poured the blood at the bottom of the altar, and sanctified it, to make reconciliation upon it*" (Leviticus 8:15). By this "*reconciliation*", not only was the altar sanctified and made holy, but it was made most holy—A Holy of holies. This expression is the same as that used to describe the inner shrine of the tabernacle where God dwelt. It is used here of the altar, which had a similar, special measure of holiness. The one was the hidden, the other the approachable Holy of holies. Then we read: "*Whatsoever toucheth the altar shall be holy*" (Exodus 29:37). By the sevenfold atoning with blood, the altar had obtained such holiness that it had the power of sanctifying everything that was laid upon it. The Israelite had no need to fear that his offering might be too small or too unworthy; the altar sanctified the gift that was laid upon it. Our Lord referred to this as a well-known fact when He asked, "*whether is greater, the gift, or the altar that sanctifieth the gift?*" (Matthew 23:19). The altar, by the sevenfold sprinkling of the blood, sanctified every offering which was laid upon it.

What a glorious, fresh light this word sheds on the power of the blood of Jesus and on His cross that is sanctified by it. As blood—proof of the surrender of the life of Christ in obedience unto death—it has power to make reconciliation and to obtain victory over sin. But lo!—Here a fresh glory of the blood is revealed to us. The cross on which it was shed is not only the altar on which Jesus was sacrificed, but it has been consecrated by that blood as an altar on which we also may be sacrificed and made acceptable to God.

It is the cross alone, as sanctified by blood (yes, sanctified to be a Holy of holies, which sanctifies everything that touches it) that has this power.

In heathen worship, people are often taught a doctrine about a cross, that by self-imposed suffering and self-sacrifice, they may become pleasing to God. But they seek a value in the sufferings themselves, as a putting to death of the flesh. They do not understand that everything that man does, whether it be suffering or sacrifice, is stained by sin and is thus incapable of really conquering sin or pleasing God. They do not understand that even the cross itself, as the means of self-sacrifice, must first be sanctified. Before the sufferings of a cross can sanctify us, it must itself first be sanctified.

For this purpose God made a most glorious provision. He caused an altar to be erected for which a sevenfold, and thus a perfect, reconciliation had been made, so that whatever touched that altar was holy. By the blood of the Son of God, the cross has become most holy—A Holy of holies, with power to sanctify us.

We know how this has been accomplished. We cannot speak or think about it too often, nor believe it or be thankful enough for it. By shedding His precious, divine blood as a sacrifice for our sin, by surrendering Himself in perfect obedience to the will of the Father, by a personal victory over sin, and by bearing our punishment and curse, Jesus has conquered sin and rendered it powerless for us also.

What Jesus did and suffered on the cross, He did and suffered as the second Adam, as our Surety, our Head. At the cross, He showed us that the only way to be freed from the flesh—in the likeness and weakness of which He came—so as to enter into the life of God and of the

Spirit was by surrendering the flesh to the righteous judgment of God. The only way into the life of God was through the death of the flesh.

But not merely did He show us that this was the only way, but by His death He obtained the right and power to enable us to walk in that very way. Our natural life is so entirely under the authority of sin that we cannot be delivered from it by any sufferings or sacrifices or endeavors of our own. But the life and sufferings of Jesus have such a divine power that by them the authority of sin has been entirely destroyed. Now everyone who seeks the way to God and to the life of God, through sacrifice and death in fellowship with Him, will find that way and be enabled to walk in it.

Through the blood of Jesus, through the perfect reconciliation and the power of an eternal life that His blood has revealed, the cross of Jesus has been sanctified forever as an altar on which alone everything that is presented to God must be offered.

The cross is an altar. We have seen that the altar is the place for slaying, the place of sacrifice. The place where the incense was offered was also called an altar. On both the altar of sacrifice and the altar of incense a fire burned. What is presented to God must first pass through death and then be consumed by fire. In its natural condition it is unclean; by death, judgment upon sin must be executed; it must be consumed by fire and in a new spiritual form borne heavenwards.

What the altar of sacrifice—what the cross—proclaims about Christ is the law in the temple of a Holy God; there is no way to God except through death, through the sacrifice of life. There is no way to God nor to heaven for us save by the cross. And the cross is not merely that cross on which we are to believe that Jesus died for our sins. No, but as the cross on which we must die. The Lord Jesus early and repeatedly warned His disciples that He must be crucified, and that they must bear their cross after Him. Each must be prepared to be crucified even as He was. He did not mean by that merely outward suffering or death. No,

He spoke of the inner self-denial, of the hating and losing the self-life as the fellowship of His cross. This was before His crucifixion.

The Holy Spirit teaches us by the apostle Paul how we are to speak about the cross after Jesus had been put to death on it:—*"I am crucified with Christ"* (Galatians 2:20); *"They that are Christ's have crucified the flesh with its affections and lusts"* (Galatians 5:24); *"God forbid that I should glory, save in the cross of our Lord Jesus Christ, by whom the world is crucified unto me, and I unto the world"* (Galatians 6:14). These three passages in the epistle to the Galatians teach us that we are not to regard the sufferings on the cross as being only the atonement of our guilt, but as the characteristic and the power of our lives. In the cross, the life of Jesus on earth attained its purpose, its climax, and its perfection. Apart from the cross He could not have been the Christ. The life of Christ from heaven bears the same characteristic in us; it is the life of the crucified One. The phrase, *"I am crucified with Christ,"* is inseparable from and coupled with the other that follows: *"Christ liveth in me"* (Galatians 2:20). Each day and each hour we must abide in the place of crucifixion. Each moment the power of the cross of Christ must work in us. We must be made conformable unto His death. Then the power of God will be manifested in us; the weakness and death of the cross is ever coupled with the life and power of God. Paul says, *"For though he [Christ] was crucified through weakness, yet he liveth by the power of God. For we also are weak in him, but we shall live with him by the power of God toward you"* (2 Corinthians 13:4).

Many Christians do not understand this. The cross in which they glory differs from that in which Paul gloried. He gloried in a cross on which not only Christ was crucified, but on which he himself was also crucified. They glory in a cross on which Christ died, but they are not willing to die on it themselves. Yet this is what God designs. The very blood that atoned for us on the cross has sanctified the cross that we might find the way of life.

Notice how clearly this distinction and this connection between the blood of atonement and the sacrifice of the flesh is taught us in the well-known passage, *"Having therefore, brethren, boldness to enter into the holiest by the blood of Jesus, by a new and living way, which he hath consecrated for us, through the veil, that is to say, his flesh...let us draw near"* (Hebrews 10:19–20, 22). *"A new and living way"* is a different thing from *"boldness...by the blood."* It is the way in which Jesus Himself walked, rending the veil of His flesh when He shed His blood. This way always passes through the rent veil of the flesh. The crucifixion and sacrifice of the flesh was the way in which the blood was shed. Everyone who obtains a share in that blood is, by that blood, brought into this way. It is the way of the cross. Nothing less than the entire sacrifice of one's self-life is the way to the life of God. The cross with its entire renunciation of self is the only altar on which we can consecrate ourselves to God. The cross has been sanctified by the blood of Jesus as the altar on which we may become a sacrifice, holy and acceptable to God.

2. THE OFFERING SANCTIFIED BY THE ALTAR

The altar is sanctified by blood, that in time it may sanctify the gift that is laid upon it. What is the gift that we have to lay on the altar? We find the answer in a word of Paul written to the Romans, *"I beseech you therefore, brethren, by the mercies of God, that ye present your bodies a living sacrifice, holy, acceptable unto God"* (Romans 12:1). The body of the victim was laid upon the altar. Christ bore our sins in His body on the tree. Our bodies are the sacrifices that we have to present to God, on the altar. The body has many members and is a wonderful union of several powers. Each of these separately, and all together, must be laid on the altar.

The body has a head—we speak of the head with the brains as the seat of understanding. The head with all its thoughts must be laid on the altar. I must consecrate my understanding entirely to the service of God, placing it entirely under His control and direction to be used by Him:

I must be *"bringing into captivity every thought to the obedience of Christ"* (2 Corinthians 10:5).

The head has its members also, the eyes and mouth and ears. By the eye, I come into touch with the visible world and its desires; the eyes must be turned away from vanity and be wholly His, to see, or not to see, according to His will. By the ear, I enter into fellowship with my fellow men. The ear must be consecrated to the Lord and is not to listen to language or conversation that pleases my flesh, but it is to be attentive to the voices that the Lord sends to me. By my mouth, I reveal what is in me, what I think and seek and will. By it I exercise an influence over others. My mouth and tongue and lips must be consecrated so that I will not speak anything except what is in accordance with God's will and to His glory. The eye, the ear, the mouth, the head, and all belonging to it must be laid on the altar to be purified and sanctified by the cross.

I must renounce every right to manage them. I must acknowledge my utter sinfulness and want of strength to control or sanctify them. I must believe that He who purchased them will accept them and guard them in the fellowship of His cross and of His entire surrender of Himself. In that faith, I must offer them to God upon the altar. The blood has sanctified the altar and made it the Holy of Holies all that touches the altar becomes holy. The act of touching is a living, spiritual, real, and, for faith, an ever-enduring thing. The reconciliation of the cross has opened the way for the fellowship of the cross. The blood has sanctified the cross as my altar.

The body also has hands and feet. The hands represent power to work. My handiwork, my business, my service, and my possessions must all be placed upon the altar to be sanctified, cleansed from sin, and consecrated to God. My feet represent my ways and my walk, the paths I choose, the companionship I cultivate, and the places that I visit. The feet, sanctified by the altar, cannot go their own way any longer. They have been presented to God to be in all things under His leading and at His service. And they must be beautiful to carry the good news and to bring help to the sorrowful and the lost. With hands and feet bound, the body must be laid upon the altar, not having the least freedom to stir, until He enables the soul to cry out, "*I am thy servant…thou hast loosed my bonds*" (Psalm 116:16).

The body has a heart, the center of life, where the blood, in which the soul dwells, flows in and out. In the heart is the meeting place of all the desires and endeavors of men, of all they will or choose, of love and hatred. The heart of Jesus was pierced on the cross. Everything that flows in or out of our heart must be laid upon the altar. I must renounce the right to seek or will anything after my own wish, to love or hate after my own desire. In the case of Jesus the cross meant: "My will is of no account: the will of God is everything"; "the will of God, cost what it may, must be done, even if it costs my life." In the smallest as well as in the greatest things God's will must be done. In nothing must my will be done—in everything God's will. That is the purpose behind the cross that Jesus sanctified as an altar for us. The will is the kingly power of the heart. It is governed by our love or hatred, and by it, in turn, the whole man is governed. When the will is on the altar, that is, on the cross, the fellowship of the cross will soon extend its power over the whole man. My will, sinful and blind; my will, condemned and freely surrendered to death; my will, put to death on the cross; my will in fellowship with Jesus living again, raised to life again, and made free; my will now entirely submitted to His leading and authority. This is the way in which the believing heart comes to understand what it means to be on the cross as on an altar. And the believer experiences that the two seemingly opposed conditions are united in a glorious union: his will bound to the cross and yet free; his will dead on the cross and yet alive. And so the truth now becomes glorious even for him, "*I am crucified with Christ…Christ liveth in me…I live by the faith*" (Galatians 2:20).

Heart and head, hands and feet together form one body. They are united in that wonderful structure of flesh in which the soul has its lodging. It was created at first to be the servant of the soul, to be kept in subjection to the guidance of the spirit; sin subverted this order. The sensual body became the seducer or tempter of the soul and has dragged the spirit down into servitude. The only way for the restoration of the order which God ordained is for the body to be placed upon the altar, the body by the Holy Spirit to be nailed to the cross. The body with its eating and drinking, with its sleeping and working, with its wonderful system of nerves by which the soul comes into contact with the world—the body must go to the altar. The power of the cross of Christ that, by the Holy Spirit, becomes at once and continuously active must have authority over the entire body. The body, with the soul and spirit dwelling in it, must become a living sacrifice to God. Thus that word of deep significance obtains its fulfillment: *"the body...for the Lord; and the Lord for the body"* (1 Corinthians 6:13).

Beloved Christian, when we gather at the Lord's Table—to meet with Him, to receive Him who was sacrificed on the cross for us—what our Lord asks us to do is to offer ourselves to Him and for Him. What will He do for us? He will receive us into the fellowship of His cross as the most glorious thing He possesses, by which He entered into the glory of the Father. In the statement concerning the altar which is sanctified by the blood so that it may in turn sanctify the gift, He points out the way and the place where we may find Him.

Are you willing to ascend the altar, the place of death? Are you willing to make the cross your abode, the place where you will pass every hour of your life in fellowship with the crucified Jesus? Or does it seem to you to be too hard to surrender yourself, your will, your life so utterly up to death, so as to bear about daily the dying of the Lord Jesus? I pray you do not think this is too hard for you. It is the only way to close fellowship with the blessed Jesus and through Him a free entrance to the eternal Father and His love.

It need not be too difficult for you! In fellowship with Jesus it will become joy and salvation. I pray you, become willing; let us ascend to the altar to die so that we may live. Or is it your fear that you are not fit to complete such a sacrifice? Listen then to the glorious comfort that the Word of God gives you today, "the altar sanctifies the gift." (See Matthew 23:19.) By the sevenfold reconciliation, even the Old Testament altar had power to sanctify every gift that was laid upon it. *"How much more shall the blood of Christ, who through the eternal Spirit offered himself without spot to God"* (Hebrews 9:14) sanctify the cross as an altar on which the sacrifice of your body may be sanctified? You have learned about the wonderful power of the precious blood, how it has conquered sin and has opened the way into "the holiest." As the blood has been sprinkled in that most holy place, before God, it has made His throne a throne of grace.

It is the very same word that is used concerning both that inner most holy place and the altar. Both are called the Holy of Holies. What the blood has accomplished by its wonderful power in the unseen Holy of holies in destroying the authority of sin in God's sight is also accomplished in the Holy of holies on which you are to be offered up. In the Holy of Holies where God dwells, the blood, by its wonderful power, has perfected everything. In your Holy of Holies where you must dwell, the blood works with no less power. Lay yourself down upon that altar. Trust the sanctifying power of the blood communicated to the altar. Believe that the blood and the cross are inseparable from the living Jesus, as High Priest, and from His Spirit, as fire. You will receive the assurance that the sanctifying of the gift by the altar is so divine and powerful that you will reckon upon a victory over all your uncleanness and weakness. Lay yourself down upon the altar as the altar of consecration and approval. The altar is the place of the blessed presence of God. Dying with Christ leads to a life with Him in the love of the Father.

It has sometimes been said that as Jesus is the Priest and Offering, He must also be the altar. There is a truth in this representation. The cross exists not apart from the crucified Christ. At the cross the living Christ is found. If this representation helps your faith, take the crucified

Christ as your altar and lay down your body with all that it contains, with all the life that dwells in it, on Him, before the Father. Then you are a living, holy sacrifice, acceptable to God. Then you will reach the full fellowship of which the Lord's Supper is the type.

"The bread which we break, is it not the fellowship of the body of Christ? The cup which we drink, is it not the fellowship of the blood of Christ?" (See 1 Corinthians 10:16.) Full fellowship with the crucified flesh and the shed blood is what He desires to give us. This fellowship is found when we give ourselves over entirely to die as He died so that we may live with Him, the crucified One. We lay ourselves on the altar, giving up ourselves to the cross, to become one by faith with the crucified Jesus.

Brethren, we have an altar; the altar sanctifies the gift. Everything that touches the altar is sanctified. I beseech you by the mercies of God that ye present your bodies a living, holy sacrifice acceptable to God.

4

FAITH IN THE BLOOD

Whom God hath set forth to be a propitiation
through faith in his blood.
—Romans 3:25

Faith in the blood of Christ is the one thing which makes the doctrines of the holiness and grace of God, of the divine and human nature of Christ, of our deliverance from sin and union with God intelligible. In the history of the kingdom of God, as well as in the experience of each believer, it becomes clear that we have in the blood of Christ the supreme revelation of the wisdom, the power, and the love of God.

Let us gather up what we have already learned and endeavor to set forth briefly and clearly its practical importance, taking by way of introduction the words of our text *"through faith in his blood."* The apostle uses these words with special reference to one particular effect of the blood—reconciliation—which, as we have seen, underlies all its other effects. And so these words may be confidently applied to everything that Scripture elsewhere teaches concerning the blood. If we obtain a better understanding and make a fuller inward appropriation of these words, our labor will not be in vain. May the Lord our God grant us the teaching of His Holy Spirit while we consider:

1. Faith to Partake in the Blessings of the Blood
2. Faith in the All-encompassing Power of the Blood

1. FAITH TO PARTAKE IN THE BLESSINGS OF THE BLOOD

"Be it unto thee according to thy faith." (See Matthew 9:29.) We know that this foundation law of the kingdom of grace is applicable to every circumstance of the spiritual life. Faith is the inner nature of the heart without which God's most glorious blessing is offered to us in vain, but by which all the fullness of God's grace can be most certainly received and enjoyed. It is therefore of great importance for us to remind ourselves of those things that are necessary for a right exercise of that faith in the precious blood. It is by that faith alone we can press through to the enjoyment of all that the blood has obtained for us. But before considering these things, it must be noted that faith is born from a sense of need.

The great event that moved heaven, earth, and hell, for which the world had to be prepared and for which it had to wait for four thousand years, the results of which will endure forever—the shedding of the blood of the Son of God on the cross—had an unspeakably great object: It was to bring about the destruction of sin itself and of its consequences.

Only he who is in agreement with this object, and who seeks to attain it, is capable of entering into the full fellowship of faith in the blessing of that blood. He who desires to be delivered only from the punishment of sin, or from sin as far as it makes him unfit for heaven, is certainly not in a condition to appropriate by a strong faith what the Word promises through the blood. But when the soul truly seeks, above everything else, to be cleansed from sin itself and to live in abiding fellowship with a holy God—it possesses the first requisites of a true faith in that blood.

The deeper the dissatisfaction with what is wrong and deficient in our spiritual lives, the stronger the longing to be really delivered from sin. The more lively the desire to have unbroken communion with God in "the holiest," so much the more is such a soul prepared to receive by faith what God promises and will bestow. Oh! If our eyes were only opened to see what God is willing to become to us; if wandering and alienation from God became entirely unbearable; if the whole soul thirsted and cried out for the living God and His love; then salvation *"through faith in his blood"* (Romans 3:25), would acquire a new meaning, and a new desire for it would be awakened. Where the sense of need exists, the first requirement for a full faith in the blood is: A spiritual knowledge of the Word of God. As surely as mere knowledge of the Word, by itself, profits but little, so surely faith cannot grow and become strong apart from the Word applied by the Holy Spirit. There are many who think that as they have always hoped in the blood as the ground of their salvation, there could not be much more for them still to learn about it. They are convinced that they are well acquainted with and hold fast the teaching of the church. They do not expect the Word to unlock anything new for them about the blood. They think so because they have so little understanding of what it means to place themselves under the guidance of the Holy Spirit, so that He, by His heavenly teaching, might inspire the well-known words or truths of Scripture with a new meaning.

They forget that it is only *"the anointing...that teacheth you of all things"* (1 John 2:27), and that *"we have received...the spirit which is of God; that we might know the things that are freely given to us of God"* (1 Corinthians 2:12). The believer who desires to understand completely the blessed power of the blood must submit entirely to the teaching of the Word through the Holy Spirit in private. He must understand that the words of God have a much wider meaning than man himself can attach to them. That the matters on which God speaks have a reality, power, and glory of which he himself can form no conception. But the Holy Spirit will teach him to understand these things—not at once, but only as he devotes time and takes trouble to learn. Believing in the rich, spiritual, living content of each Word of God, the learner must understand that "the blood of the Son of God" is a subject the glory of which God alone knows, and He alone can reveal. He must believe it is possible for each facet that is ascribed to the blood to be brought about by a manifestation of divine power that is beyond our conception. In this attitude of mind, he should meditate on what one portion of Scripture says about the blood, and then what another portion says, so that the Holy Spirit may apply to his soul something of its life-giving power. It is only by such a use of the Word, in dependence upon the teaching of the Holy Spirit, that faith can be strengthened so as to recognize and receive what the blood has to bestow.

By this means we realize how necessary it is to devote time to these things. Time must be found for meditation on the Word in private, so that it may sink into the heart. To read a portion, to get hold of a fresh thought, and then to go away in the hope that a blessing will follow is of little use. The soul must give the Word time, in silence before God, to get fixed in the heart. Otherwise it will be driven away again by the rush of the world. The thought may remain, but there will be no power. Time must be given, not merely occasionally, but regularly and persistently. Day after day, perhaps week after week, I must place myself under and give myself up to the Word that I desire to appropriate. It can become in reality the possession of my soul only by obtaining a lodging place in, and by becoming part of, my spiritual being. It is thus *"faith cometh...by the word of God"* (Romans 10:17).

Faith is the ear that hears and receives the Word of God. It listens attentively to understand what God says. Faith is the eye which seeks to place before itself, as an object of vital importance, what would otherwise remain only a thought. Faith thus sees the invisible. It observes the things which are not seen. It is the sure evidence of these things. Faith is accustomed to surround itself with, and to dwell in the midst of, those things that the Word leads the understanding to regard as heavenly realities. So it seeks to behold, in Spirit, the blood being brought into heaven and sprinkled upon the throne and, by the Spirit, sprinkled upon the soul, with powerful results. But faith is not only an ear and eye to ascertain; it is also a *hand* and *mouth* to receive. What it hears from the Word, what it in Spirit beholds, it appropriates to itself. Faith surrenders itself to the impression produced by what is heard, places itself under the influence of invisible objects, until they have secured for themselves a lodging in the heart, in their heavenly, life-giving power.

Faith accepts it as a certainty that what the Word of God says, the power of God is prepared to make objectively real.

It is in fellowship with the Lord Jesus Himself that faith can be exercised and strengthened. It is a matter too little understood, that God bestows salvation upon us in no other way than in—not just through, but in—the Savior. The living Jesus is salvation. He who gave and now imparts His blood, it is in Him that we must daily find our life and our salvation. Further, it is only in living in direct fellowship with Him that our faith can increase and triumph. Many Christians take great pains in endeavoring to reach a life of full faith by earnest association with the Word, or by straining all their powers to believe, and yet they see but little fruit as the result of their efforts. The reason often is that, in studying the Word, and in trying to believe, they have not first of all found rest themselves in the love of the Savior.

Faith in God is an act of the spiritual life. It is Christ who is our life and who imparts faith to us. He does this, however, not as an act or gift separate from Himself. It is in fellowship with Him that faith is active. He is *"the author and finisher of our faith"* (Hebrews 12:2). Those who walk with Him learn from Him to exercise faith. In the face of Jesus, the light that leads to the *"full assurance of faith"* (Hebrews 10:22) is always found. To gaze upon His face, to sit still at His feet that the light of His love may shine upon the soul is a sure way of obtaining a strong faith. He who longs for such a faith in order to come to the knowledge of the full power of the blood needs only to practice this fellowship.

The shedding of His blood was the proof of His unspeakable love towards us. *"He gave himself for us, that he might redeem us from all iniquity, and purify unto himself a peculiar people"* (Titus 2:14). His blood is the power by which He takes possession of us for Himself, to sanctify us. All that is necessary for the more powerful operation of the blood in us is that faith in it should become wider, brighter, and stronger. He who longs for such a full faith will find it only, but find it certainly, in fellowship with Jesus. It is His work to impart the blood; it is His work also to increase faith. Let there only be an undivided surrender to the Lord Jesus, the sacrifice of the "self"-life—"I"—in order to walk with Him; in that walk unbelief will wither.

This undivided surrender, however, is indispensable. True faith always includes entire surrender. To believe with the whole heart means to surrender with the whole heart to Jesus in whom life and salvation are. The will and the law of the Lord Jesus are inseparable from His person and from His love. We cannot know nor receive Him without knowing and receiving His will: obedience is the one sure characteristic of the surrender of faith. Faith that is not coupled with obedience is an imagination or pretense; there is not a true surrender to Christ. But the faith in which this true surrender is found presses ever on to a deeper insight into what the blood means and to the experience of what it can do.

2. FAITH IN THE ALL-ENCOMPASSING POWER OF THE BLOOD

We will not repeat what has already been said about the different effects of the blood, but will point out some special characteristics of the way in which the blood accomplishes its work. Faith, however, must first be aroused to recognize and appropriate the fact that the blessed effects of the blood make all things possible, are ever enduring, and all inclusive.

All things are possible: The blood has a divine power to produce results in us today.

We have several times spoken of the wonderful power that the blood of Jesus manifested immediately after He had shed it. It was by that blood that Jesus, in His holy, triumphal march, broke open the doors of death and Hades and carried its prisoners out with Him. That, as Conqueror, He might see the doors of heaven thrown open for the blood—and that He might take possession of the Holy of holies of God on our behalf. The blood works today with a similar wonderful power to that which the blood manifested then in making reconciliation for sin, in removing its curse, in opening the holiest, in restoring fellowship with God. With the very same power that was manifested then in those supreme things—concerning sin and its authority, concerning God and His law, concerning hell and heaven—with the very same power, the divine blood works now when sprinkled on a single soul. That its divine power in our individual hearts is too little experienced we must confess. But this is because of our unbelief. If it were not for this unbelief, the mere thought of being ransomed and cleansed by the blood of God's own Son would cause our souls to leap for joy and to overflow with love. Would not every exercise of faith in the blood cause the sense of the favor and nearness of God and the glory of deliverance from the curse and dominion of sin to flow through the soul? But, alas! We may hear and think and sing about the blood, while it exercises almost no influence over us. Even the very thought that the blood always manifests such wonderful divine power seems strange and unreal to many, and so no wonderful work is done in us because of unbelief.

Our faith must be quickened to expect the all-conquering power of the blood. Even if a change in our feelings does not come at once, nor any sensation of new blessing, let us commence in perfect quietness to fix our hearts on these truths of God. When the blood becomes effective through the Spirit, it operates with the divine power either for reconciliation or union with God or sanctification. Let us believe and still believe and ever keep on believing in the infinite power of the blood. Such faith will not be in vain. Although it may not be in the way, nor at the time we expected, we shall be brought into a new and deeper experience of salvation *"through faith in his blood"* (Romans 3:25). Let us but seek with our whole heart to hold fast the truth: what the blood does, it does with a divine power.

Next to its power to make all things possible, our faith must be assured that the power of the blood endures forever.

We have already seen on what foundation faith is grounded. By the eternal Spirit, the blood was once for all offered. By the eternal High Priest, it is administered in the power of an endless life. The power of the blood is eternally active. There is no single moment in which the blood is not exerting its full power. In the heavenly Holy of Holies where the blood is before the throne, everything exists in the power of eternity, without cessation or diminution. All activities in the heavenly temple are on our behalf, and the effects are conveyed to us by the Holy Spirit. He is Himself the eternal Spirit and has been bestowed on us to make us partakers of all that has been or will be done for us by our Lord Jesus. He is able to make us partakers, in a very powerful and blessed way, of the continuous activities of the blood that never for one moment cease.

In the morning before you go out to work and to meet the distractions of the day, commit yourself to Him who ever remains the same, that He may reveal in you the ever-living activity of His blood, and He will do it. During the hours of business, when you can think of nothing else, the blessed results of the sprinkling of the blood and the nearness of God, of cleansing, of victory over sin, will be made yours. Our activity of faith must be an abiding thing, but not in the sense that we must anxiously take care to think about it every moment. But in such a way that we, from the depths of our souls, cherish a quiet and steadfast confidence that eternal redemption has taken possession of us and holds us fast by its heavenly activity if only we are trustful. Thank God, we need not fear. Each moment, without ceasing, we may live here below in the enjoyment of the blessing that the blood has procured for us, because the effects of the blood are ever-enduring.

Not less are we to believe in the all-embracing, all-penetrating power of the blood.

When the priests were separated to their ministry, the blood was placed upon the tip of the ear, on the thumb of the hand, and on the toe of the foot. Possession was taken of the entire man for God. All his powers were sanctified: his ear to listen to and for God; his hand to work by and for God; his foot to walk with God and to go out in His service. In the case of the believer, the precious blood of Christ will exercise a similar authority over every power, to sanctify it for the service of the Lord.

Christians have often had to complain about a divided life: there are certain portions of life or of work that are a hindrance in a walk with God. The only way to obtain deliverance from this is to see that the blood covers everything. *"Almost all things are by the law purged with blood"* (Hebrews 9:22). The entire person of the believer, with all his circumstances and affairs, must be brought into the Holy of holies.

It is evident that, to enjoy such an experience, a most complete surrender to the Lord is necessary. The priest who was marked by blood on the ear, hand, and foot, so that all the activities of these members might be sanctified, had to recognize that he had been separated to the service of God. The believer must give himself up no less wholly to be and live only for Jesus. In each relationship of his life, his home, his business, commercial or political affairs, he must give himself up to be led by the Holy Spirit, to live according to the law of God and for His glory. Then, the blood in its reconciling, cleansing, and sanctifying power will embrace everything. The peace of God and the consciousness of His nearness will reveal itself in all things, by the power of the heavenly life. He will experience the completeness of his deliverance from the authority of sin, of his liberty to enter upon a walk in the light and love of a Holy God. But always on this one condition: everything must be brought into the Holy of holies and set right there. The whole life must be spent there, for that is where the blood is and where it exercises its power. This again, is by faith; faith that is absorbed in what the blood has accomplished in the Holy of holies, and what power it now exercises there. And that faith maintains, on the authority of the Word, that all this power can be brought into uninterrupted contact with the personal life.

And then, in proportion as the believer learns in his own experience how far-reaching the effects of the all-including blood are, his heart will be opened to long for a widespread experience of the power of the blood in the world around him.

"For it pleased the Father that in him should all fullness dwell; and, having made peace through the blood of his cross, by him to reconcile all things unto himself…whether they be things in earth, or things in heaven" (Colossians 1:19–20). The power of the blood avails for every creature, for those also who have *"counted the blood of the covenant, wherewith he was sanctified, an unholy thing"* (Hebrews 10:29), and for those who are *"denying the Lord that bought them"* (2 Peter 2:1). The experience of what the blood can accomplish for those who believe will teach them to regard their fellow men as living under the tender mercy of God, under redemption, and under the call to salvation through the precious blood. It will fill them with an irresistible impulse to devote their lives, which have been bought by the blood, to be fellow workers with God. They have been consecrated to bear witness to the blood by word and by prayer, that the blood may have the honor that belongs to it. *"Ye were not redeemed with corruptible things, such as silver or gold…but with the precious blood of Christ"* (1 Peter 1:18–19) will become for them the one all-inclusive thing to which they devote their lives. A Christian writer has testified that the insight into what the blood can do in its ever-cleansing power was the beginning of a new experience in her spiritual life. Sometime later she wrote: "I see more and more clearly that it is only by the abiding indwelling of the Holy Spirit that this hidden power of the blood can be revealed and experienced." May our lives also be under the teaching of the Holy Spirit that He may constantly keep us also in the heavenly blessedness and joy that the blood has procured for us.

5

THE BLOOD OF THE LAMB

These are they which came out of great tribulation, and have washed their robes, and made them white in the blood of the Lamb.
—Revelation 7:14

We have already, in our meditations on the precious blood of Christ, considered the question of what it really is that bestows such value on the blood. Scripture has given us an answer from more than one viewpoint. It was because of His eternal Godhead, His true manhood, His infinite love, His perfect obedience. In all these we found a reason why His blood exercised such an immeasurable power with God and men.

The Scripture quoted above calls us to the consideration of this subject from still another side.

The new name given to the blood here is *"the blood of the Lamb"* (Revelation 12:11). We need to learn what the peculiar characteristics and results of the blood are that can only be revealed by the expression, the blood of the Lamb.

When our Lord Jesus is called the Lamb of God, there are two leading thoughts that are bound up with that name. One is that He is the Lamb of God because He was slain as a sacrifice for sin. The second is that He was lamb-like, gentle, and patient. The first emphasizes the work that He as a Lamb had to accomplish; the second emphasizes the gentleness that characterized Him as Lamb. The first of these views is the more general one. We have often had the opportunity of speaking about the value of the blood from that point of view, as for instance in the chapter on "The Altar and the Blood." The second has too often been lost sight of. Let us on this occasion fix our attention specifically on it, in order that we may obtain our share of the rich blessing that is contained in it for us. Taking as our point of view the inner nature that inspired our Lord as the Lamb of God, we shall see that it is just this that makes the blood so precious—it is the blood of the gentle Lamb of God.

We shall consider what it means, that in heaven they praise the blood as the blood of the Lamb.

1. This Bestows upon the Blood Its Value.

2. This Reveals the True Nature of Redemption

3. This Assures Us of a Perfect Salvation.

1. THE BLOOD OF THE LAMB: THIS BESTOWS UPON THE BLOOD ITS VALUE

When Jesus was on earth He said, *"Come unto me...learn of me; for I am meek and lowly in heart: and ye shall find rest unto your souls"* (Matthew 11:28–29). He did not mention meekness as one of several other virtues that were to be learned from Him, but as *the* one that was His chief characteristic, the one that they must learn if they were to find rest for their souls. He who takes the trouble to understand this aright will have a vision of the true inwardness of the work by which our redemption has been obtained.

The Lord came to deliver us from sin. In what does sin really consist? It exists in self-exaltation and in pride. This was the sin of the angels who fell. They were created to find their life in God alone. They began to view themselves and the wonderful gifts that God had bestowed upon them with pride. They began to consider that their dependence upon God and subjection to Him were a humiliation, a curtailment of their liberty and enjoyment. They exalted themselves against God, seeking their own glory instead of that of God. That moment they fell into the abyss of destruction. Pride and self-seeking changed them from angels into demons, cast them from heaven to hell, turned the light and the blessedness of heaven into the darkness and flames of hell. When God created a new world with man created for it, to repair the destruction wrought by the fall of the angels, Satan came to lead man into the same opposition to God. The temptation that the serpent presented to the woman was intended simply to draw man away from subjection to God. Along with the words that Satan whispered into Eve's ear, he breathed into her soul the deadly poison of pride. And since man listened to him, self-exaltation became in his case, also, the root of all sin and sorrow. His life is made up of self-love, self-will, and self-pleasing. Self, "I", is the idol he serves. Self is a thousand-headed monster that, as self-seeking, self-pleasing, self-confidence and self-esteem is the fruitful mother of all the sin and misery that is to be found in the world. The authority of Satan is exercised over, the fire of hell burns in, all that belongs to "self," "I," "pride"; and the soul becomes consumed with a thirst that can never be quenched.

If the Lord Jesus was to become our true Savior one thing was most necessary—He must deliver us from ourselves. He must bring about a death to self, I, to the self-life, and lead us again to live for God, so that we may "live no more to ourselves." *"None of us liveth to himself"* (Romans 14:7). This is the only way by which man can become truly blessed. And there is, further, no other means by which this way can be prepared for us, except by the Lord Jesus opening the path for us, obtaining a new life for us, and imparting it to us. Of that life, denial of self and self-humiliation should be the chief characteristic and the inner blessedness. So that in this way God might again take up His rightful place and become our All-in-all in that new life.

This is the reason why the Lord Jesus had to come into the world as the Lamb of God. He had to bring back again to earth the meekness and lowliness of heart in which true submission to God is manifested. It was no longer to be found on earth. He brought it from heaven. In heaven He humbled Himself as Son before the Father that He might be sent as a servant into the world. He humbled Himself to become man. As man He humbled Himself to the death of the cross. As *"the Lamb of*

God" (Revelation 12:11) He denied Himself with a heavenly meekness that surpasses all our thoughts to become a servant of God and man, that He might please God and man. This was the inner quality that inspired Him and constituted the true nature of His sufferings, which made Him a complete victor over sin. It was as the *"Lamb of God"* that He took away the sin of the world. This is what bestows such virtue upon His blood. He inflicted a deadly wound on sin, gaining the victory in His own person. He subjected Himself to the will of God. And through His whole life, under the severest temptations, He sacrificed Himself for the glory of God with a lowliness and patience and meekness that were the delight of the Father and of all the holy angels. He did all this as *"the Lamb of God."* He crowned all this when He shed His blood as *"the Lamb of God"* for the reconciliation of sin and for the cleansing of our souls. This is why praise is offered in heaven for His blood, as the blood of *"the Lamb of God."* This is why the Father has placed Him *"in the midst of the throne"* as the *"Lamb* [that] *had been slain"* (Revelation 5:6). This is why believers, in tender astonishment and love, glorying in the *"blood of the Lamb,"* praise His meekness and lowliness as their greatest joy and their one desire. As *"the blood of the Lamb"* it possesses virtue and power for complete redemption.

2. THE BLOOD OF THE LAMB: THIS REVEALS THE TRUE NATURE OF REDEMPTION

The Lord Jesus came to do in His own person what we could not do. He also came to make us, who did not possess it, partakers of the treasure that He had procured. His lowliness is the gift that He brought from heaven. His lowliness is what He wishes to bestow upon us. And as the blood was the manifestation and the result of the divine meekness in Him, so it is also in us the manifestation and result of our contact with the blood.

Our fellowship in His blood, what is it but fellowship in His death? And His death was only the culmination of His humiliation and sacrifice. It was a proof that there was no other way by which to attain to the fullness of the life of God—resurrection life—except through death. And so the blood—as a fellowship in His death, as a participation of the inner power of His death—calls us to give ourselves over to death through His humiliation and self-sacrifice, as the only way to the life of God. A Christian who thinks that he is trusting in the blood often gives way to pride, self-will and self-exaltation. But if he only really knew that *"the blood of the Lamb"* is at work in him every moment, in living power, then he would recognize in this fact a decided call, coupled with a supply of power to enable him to manifest his faith in that blood with the meekness of Christ.

This is a subject upon which the attention of Christians must be much more fixed than is generally the case. We must learn that there is no way to heaven except by lowliness, by entirely dying to our pride, and by living entirely in the lowliness of Jesus.

Pride is from hell: it is the poison of Satan in our blood. Pride must die or nothing of heaven can live in you. Under the banner of this truth you must surrender yourself to the Spirit of the meek and lowly Lamb, to *"the Lamb of God,"* the victor over all pride. Each exercise of faith in *"the Lamb of God,"* each act of thanksgiving for the love and the blessedness brought to you by it, ought to powerfully encourage you to desire supremely to know and to manifest the humility of *"the Lamb of God."* All your worship of God from a heart cleansed and saturated by the blood ought to strengthen you in the blessed certainty that where *"the blood of the Lamb"* is, there He is Himself in His meekness, to sanctify the heart as a temple of God.

We must not only recognize that this meek spirit, which in God's sight is of great value, must be the object of our desire and effort, but we must believe that it is really possible for us to obtain a share in it. Jesus Christ is the second Adam, who really restores what the first Adam lost. Our pride and self-seeking, everything that self does or produces, all the sorrow that arises from our self-will and self-love is only a continuation of that first turning away from God, when Adam fell under the authority of Satan. There can be no thought of any redemption or approach to God without an entire turning back to a life of decided dependence, humility, and submission to God. The only way for redemption from the condition of pride is by death; dying to the life of self, the surrender of the self-life to death, to make room for the new life. And there is nothing in the entire universe that can make that death possible for us, and work out a new life in us, except such a heavenly lowliness as *"the Lamb of God"* brought from heaven, and which He made transferrable to us by His death. What He was when He died, such He was when He arose from the dead. As the *"Lamb of God"* He is the second Adam, our Head, and He lives to bestow His Spirit upon us. Yes, by His Spirit the Lamb of God will certainly bestow this meekness and will work it out in the heart of everyone who surrenders his life entirely to the power of the blood. We have already seen that the shedding of the blood was followed by the shedding forth of the Spirit, and that the Spirit and the blood bear witness together. Where the blood reaches there also is the Spirit. John saw the Lamb in the midst of the throne standing as if slain, *"having seven eyes, which are the seven Spirits of God sent forth into all the earth"* (Revelation 5:6). The Spirit works as the Spirit of the Lamb. He works with a hidden, but divine power, breathing into the heart of His own people that which is the divine glory of the Lamb—His meekness.

Do you desire to understand how these effects of the blood and the Spirit may be experienced? Do you complain that you know but little about them? Do you fear that in you perhaps it may never be possible? You may learn how it is possible, if you are a believer, that the Spirit is in you as a seed of God. That seed appears small and dead; its life-power is hidden and not yet active. Begin to esteem that seed of the divine nature. Keep calm, that you may quietly believe that the Spirit is in you. Believe that the gentleness of the Lamb is also in you as a seed, a hidden power of the Spirit. Begin in that faith to pray to God to strengthen you by His

Spirit in the inner man. Take any hour of the day—say nine o'clock—when you will (even if it is but for one moment) send up a prayer for the bestowment upon you of your inheritance, the meekness and gentleness of the Lamb. Cultivate the virtue of welcoming everything that calls for or helps you to humility. You may rely upon it that the hitherto hidden seed, the Spirit of Jesus, will open out and spring up on you. And it will become your experience that the blood of the Lamb has brought you into contact with a lowliness which is powerful and blessed beyond all thought.

3. THE BLOOD OF THE LAMB: THIS ASSURES US OF A PERFECT SALVATION

We would have thought that in calling our Lord "the Lamb" this name would have been used only in respect to His humiliation in His earthly life. Yet in Scripture it is most used in reference to His glory in heaven. John saw Him stand, as a Lamb that has been slain, in the midst of the throne. The four living creatures and the four and twenty elders and the hosts of heaven praise Him as the Lamb who purchased us unto God by His blood. "*Salvation to our God...and to the Lamb*" Revelation 7:10). It is the Lamb who executes judgment, who conquered Satan and all his power. The Lamb is the Temple and the Lamp of the New Jerusalem. It is from beneath the throne of God and of the Lamb that the river of the water of life flows. In heaven, through eternity, the Lamb is all in all. He is the glory and joy of heaven. Eternity will reecho the song of His praise: "*Worthy is the Lamb that was slain to receive power, and riches, and wisdom, and strength, and honor, and glory, and blessing*" (Revelation 5:12).

And why is all this? "*Thou art worthy...for thou wast slain, and hast redeemed us to God by thy blood*" (Revelation 5:9). It is the blood of the Lamb that bestows this glory upon Him. By His own blood He has entered into the Holy of holies and is seated at the right hand of the Majesty in heaven. His blood has accomplished this. Because He humbled Himself to death, therefore, God has so highly exalted Him. As *"the Lamb of God"* (John 1:29), meek and lowly of heart, He glorified God even to the pouring out of His life. Therefore, He is esteemed to be worthy of being praised forever by the song of the universe. *"Salvation to our God which sitteth upon the throne, and unto the Lamb"* (Revelation 7:10). The blood has brought this about.

The blood will be effective for us also. All on whom the precious blood has been sprinkled must come to that place where the Lamb is and where the blood is, where all those who have been bought and cleansed by the blood will honor and praise the Lamb forever. All on whom the precious blood has been sprinkled will come to the place where the Lamb will lead them to the fountains of living water and will perfect the salvation that He began in them, as they obtain a share in the marriage supper of the Lamb and forever worship God where the Lamb is the Temple and the Light. Yes, certainly the blood of the Lamb is the only, but the certain, pledge of a perfect salvation. And that is not only in eternity, but here on earth in this life. The more we meditate upon the glory of eternity and contemplate the unspeakable blessedness which He bestows, the more settled will our faith become that the blood that accomplishes such incomprehensible things *there* is able to affect *here also* a heavenly and thought-surpassing power is us.

Yes, the blood of the Lamb that was powerful enough to destroy sin, to open heaven for sinners, and to bring their salvation to such perfection, that blood surely has power to cleanse our hearts, to saturate them, and fill them with all the power and joy that the Lamb on the throne will, even here, pour out upon us.

That blood is powerful to cleanse us from pride, to sanctify us with the holiness of the Lamb, His heavenly gentleness and humility. In Him we see humility crowned by God and all-conquering gentleness exalted to the throne. He is able to reveal this in our hearts. The blood of the Lamb: the pledge of a perfect salvation! Oh, that we in deep astonishment and worship might let our hearts be filled with this truth. Our faith must take time to nourish itself by the reality of what is revealed to us, the reality of what takes place in heaven today and shall continue forever, the reality of the powerful activities that stream forth from the blood here on earth every moment. In that faith, we must present ourselves before Him, who Himself has cleansed us by His blood and made us kings and priests. He Himself will keep alive in us an effective application of the blood.

Learn, I pray you, that here is your way to eternal blessedness. Let each contact with the blood be contact with the Lamb, more particularly with His gentleness and meekness. Let your faith touch just the hem of His garment and power will go out from Him. "Self" is our one sin and sorrow; wholly and always denial of self is our only redemption.

Fellowship with the death of the Lamb of God is our only entrance into the life that He bestows. If only we knew what a sweet, heavenly, heart-changing power there is in humility like that of the Lamb of God, which moved Him to give His blood. How this would drive the poison of Satan and pride out of our fallen nature; how this would bestow on us the water of life, to extinguish the fire of our self-seeking! Would we not rather sacrifice everything than fail to possess it in full measure? How we should praise the blood of the Lamb as the revelation, the impartation, and the eternal glory of humility!

6

THE BLOOD-BOUGHT MULTITUDE

And they sung a new song, saying, Thou art worthy to take the book,
and to open the seals thereof: for thou wast slain,
and hast redeemed us to God by thy blood out of every kindred,
and tongue, and people, and nation.
—Revelation 5:9

When we lay our gifts for the work of the Lord upon His altar, it should not be done from mere custom, or without serious thought. Every penny that comes into His treasury has a value corresponding to the intention with which it is offered to Him. Only true love to Him and His work transforms our gifts into spiritual offerings. It would be well for us to learn what God thinks and says about missionary work if we are to think and act according to His will.

The work of the missionary is always a work of faith—faith that is sure evidence of things man cannot see. It is guided in everything by what is seen or heard in the unseen world. The outstanding value of missionary work lies in the fact that it is a work of faith. It has always been something beyond mere human comprehension, for mere human wisdom cannot understand it, and the natural man has no love for it. He cannot imagine how it is possible for a raw heathen to be tamed and renewed by nothing save the message of the love of God in Christ.

The men who in all ages have stood at the head of the great missionary undertakings have received from heaven, by the Word and Spirit of God, the light and power needed for their work. It was the eye of faith fixed on Jesus as King that opened their hearts to receive His command

and His promise, in which they found both the impulse and the courage for their work.

Our text tells us of a vision of things in "the heavenlies" that sheds the light of eternity upon the work of missions. We hear the song of the redeemed who praise the Lamb that He had redeemed them to God by His blood. And in their song, that which is mentioned as of prime importance after the praise of the Lamb—or rather that is one part of that praise—is the fact that they were gathered together out of *"every kindred, and tongue, and nation."* This is mentioned in praise of the power that the blood had exercised. There was no kindred, nor nation, which had not its representatives among those redeemed by the blood of the Lamb. There was no division of language or nationality of which the breach had not been healed. All were united in one spirit of love, and in one body, before the throne.

What else is that vision except a heavenly revelation of the high calling and glorious result of mission work? Without mission work that vision could not have become fact, nor could that song have been sung. In that song is set forth the divine right of missionary work and the heavenly supply that empowers it. Every time a friend of missions, or the people of God, hear the notes of that song, they receive a loud call to fresh courage and renewed consecration and to fresh joy in the glorious work of gathering together the *"great multitude, which no man could number"* (Revelation 7:9).

In these chapters on "the power of the blood," we have hitherto fixed our attention chiefly on its effects in the individual soul. It is right that we should now, for once, inquire into the far-reaching extent and wonderfully powerful effects of His blood in the world.

Missionary work will appear in a new light to us when we see in what relationship it stands to the blood that is so precious to us, and we shall be strengthened to serve the missionary cause, if we understand that the power behind it is nothing less than "the power of the blood of

Jesus." We shall learn that in order to carry on that work we must ever regard it as work of faith; a work that receives its recommendation, not from what is seen on earth, but from what is heard from heaven.

In order to understand this better, let us consider mission work:

IN THE BLOOD THAT BESTOWS ITS POWER

It is in this that faith finds her power. In the song of the great multitude gathered by missionary activity, we hear that it is the blood of the Lamb by which they were redeemed, to which they owe their participation in salvation. Let us consider how that blood is, in truth, the power of the missionary movement. It is that blood alone that bestows the courage, awakens the love, and provides the weapons to which missions owe their victory.

The blood bestows courage. How else could weak men and women have dared to attempt to attack the power of Satan in heathendom and rob him of his prey? If the thought had come from the great statesmen, or from the warriors who had conquered the peoples of the heathen world and intended in this matter also to conquer them, or if it had come from men of learning, who believe in the power of knowledge and civilization, then we might perhaps have understood it. But no, these men were generally the fiercest opponents of the work. The thought was conceived and cherished in the quietness of hidden circles, of those who were of no consideration or influence in the world.

What was it then that gave them the needed courage? It was nothing else than the blood of Christ and faith in the power of that blood. They saw in the Word of God that God had "*set forth* [Christ] *to be a propitiation through faith in his blood*" (Romans 3:25) a propitiation "*also for the sins of the whole world*" (1 John 2:2). They saw that that blood availed for every kindred and tongue and nation. It was granted to them to perceive that the blood had been carried into heaven and is now set down before the throne as the ransom for the deliverance of souls for whom it had been lawfully paid. They heard the voice of the Father to the Son, *"Ask of me and I will give thee the heathen for thine inheritance"* (Psalm 2:8). They knew that no power of hell could prevent the Lord Jesus from reaching all those for whom His blood was shed. Satan was conquered by that blood and was cast out of heaven; that blood had power to conquer him on earth also and to deliver his prisoners out of his hand. By the sprinkling of that blood in heaven, the power of sin was forever broken. And all that could hinder the outflowing of the love or blessing of God towards the most unworthy was removed, and the way opened for His people, through faith and prayer, to obtain heavenly power, so that in their weakness they might perform wondrous things. They knew with certainty that the blood of Jesus Christ, God's Son, was the pledge that men from every people and tongue should bow before Jesus.

The blood that bestowed courage to believe this awakened also love to act on that belief. We, here on earth, speak of blood relationship as being the strongest that exists. The blood of Jesus awakens the sentiment of a heavenly blood relationship, not only among those who are already cleansed, but also for those for whom that blood was shed. The blood of Christ expresses the surrender of love, even to death. It is, therefore, the death of selfishness, and opens the fountain of an eternal love in the heart.

The more deeply the believer lives in the power of the blood of Christ, the more clearly he views mankind, even the heathen, in the light of redemption. That the blood has been shed for the most degraded bestows a value on every man and forms the band of a love that embraces all.

The confidence of faith—that the blood will obtain its recompense out of every tongue and nation—should be followed by a purpose of love. I, who myself owe everything to that blood, must bear witness to it and make it known to those who have not yet heard of it. The blood that is for all is also for me. By faith in that word the soul obtains a share in its blessing. The blood that is for me is also for all. By faith in that word, love for my fellow man burns and sacrifices self to reveal the power of the blood to others. Yes, that blood is the power of mission work, for it is those who live in the full fellowship of that blood who are driven by the love of Christ to carry the tidings to others of that glorious portion that belongs to them. The friends of missions have need of nothing less than love with its super-earthly power. It is this love alone, brought down to earth, which is able to embrace the wretched ones and to persevere when all hope seems lost. There are mission fields where God's servants have labored for twenty or thirty years without seeing any fruit for their labor, and supporters of societies in Europe have asked if it did not appear to be God's will not to open a door there. But love of souls enabled them to persevere, and later on a rich and blessed harvest has been reaped.

The blood is at the same time the weapon used by missionaries in the strife. It is not enough that the believer has courage and love for the work, and power to begin it and persevere with it. Where can he obtain power to really touch the darkened heart so as to incline and to move it to forsake the gods of its forefathers, to receive the teaching of the cross along with the sacrifice of everything that the natural man desires, and listen to the call to a heavenly and spiritual life? That power the missionary movement finds in the blood of the cross.

The history of missions supplies the most touching proofs of this. Thus, we learn that in the beginning of mission work in certain countries the missionaries thought that they must first teach the people about God and His law, about sin and righteousness. They did that for more than twenty years without awakening them out of their deadly carelessness. On a certain evening, a brother read a portion of the New Testament that he had translated to a single heathen who had visited him. It was the story of the agony in Gethsemane. "Read that again," said the man. When he had reread it, he asked the missionary what it meant. When the missionary began to explain the sufferings and death of God's Son, the heathen's heart was broken. He was immediately enabled to believe, and then followed a glorious work. The blood of the cross had won the victory.

It is more than one hundred years since that occurred. But every mission field supplies proof that what the wisdom of this world cannot do has been done through simple men and women, by their message about the blood of the Lamb. And it is because there are thousands of God's children who heartily believe this that they will not allow themselves, by any means, to be turned away from their love for the glorious, precious work of missions. It is by this work that *"a great multitude, which no man can number"* (Revelation 7:9) is gathered together to sing the new song in praise of the Lamb that redeemed them to God by His blood. Beloved Christians, there is one question that presses itself upon all of us who profess to be redeemed by the blood of Jesus. The question is "What is the value of that blood to us?"

He who does not love Jesus cannot understand mission work, for he knows nothing about the secret blessing of missions and the redemption of souls. Mission work is the work of eternity; therefore, it is a work of faith. Just as the Lord Jesus Himself was despised when He was upon earth and not esteemed, yet the glory of God was in Him, so also is it with mission work. God is with it; He is in it. Do not allow yourselves to be misled by its outward weakness and deficiencies to misunderstand it. Live for it; give to it; work for it; speak for it; pray for it. If you are a Christian, be also a friend of missions. He who knows the power of the blood in his own heart cannot be anything else than a friend of missions.

I pray you, by the blood of the Lamb, by your hope of one day joining in the song of the Lamb, by your hope of being welcomed by the unnumbered multitude as a companion in redemption, live as one of the witnesses of the blood of Jesus. As you live only by the blood, live also only for the blood, and give yourself no rest till all His purchased ones know of His glory.

7

"WHEN I SEE THE BLOOD"

The blood shall be to you for a token upon the houses where ye are: and when I see the blood, I will pass over you, and the plague shall not be upon you to destroy you, when I smite the land of Egypt.
—Exodus 12:13

The story of the Passover is well known to us all. The Lord was about to lead His people out of Egypt and, in the night of their departure, to inflict judgment upon Egypt. The Lord considered Israel as His firstborn son among the nations. Egypt had transgressed against Him by ill treatment of this firstborn son, and so punishment must fall on "the firstborn" of Egypt. In every house the firstborn would be smitten by the destroying angel, who, at midnight, would pass through the land of Egypt. The Egyptians and the Israelites in many cases dwelt near one another, and so a sign must be set on the door of every Israelite house, that the destroying angel might not enter there to slay. That sign was to be the blood of a lamb, slain by the father of the family, according to the commandment given by God. *"The blood shall be to you for a token"*—so God had said. It was to be a sign, an assurance by which the Israelite might have entire confidence concerning the safety of his family. It would be a sign also before God of the spiritual condition of the father of the house regarding his obedience of faith through which God would spare his house: *"When I see the blood, I will pass over you."*

We know why it is that the blood, and nothing else, was established by God as a sign. Although Israel was God's people, they were also, alas, a sinful people. As far as sin was concerned, if it was to be treated as it deserved, then the destroying angel must exercise judgment on Israel also. But the blood was to be a token of redemption. The death of the

Lamb that was slain was considered as taking the place of the death that man had earned by his sin. The redemption of Israel, however, was not to take place simply by the exercise of power, but according to law and righteousness. Therefore, the punishment of the sin of each Israelite home had to be warded off by the blood of the paschal lamb. (The paschal lamb is the lamb slaughtered on the eve of Passover. It is a foreshadowing of the paschal lamb that is Jesus Christ.) Each father of a household, by the sprinkling of blood on the door of his house, had to give proof of his recognition of his sinfulness and need of deliverance. He showed his confidence in God's promise of redemption, by his willing obedience to God's command. All this was in a remarkable way represented by the blood of the paschal lamb. In the New Testament we read: *"Christ our passover is sacrificed for us"* (1 Corinthians 5:7). The outstanding name that He bears in heaven, namely, the Lamb of God, refers chiefly to what He, as our paschal lamb, has done for our redemption. And if we wish to declare in the simplest manner how His blood obtains our salvation, then we cannot teach it in a better way than by the type of the Passover in Egypt. Up till now, in explaining the power of Jesus' blood in these chapters, we have dealt chiefly with believers. We now address ourselves to the simplest and most unlearned in spiritual things, to those who, as yet, understand nothing about this blood. May God grant to them knowledge of the preciousness of the blood of Christ by the glorious type supplied by the Passover!

Attention is drawn to:

1. The Danger to Be Averted by the Blood

2. The Deliverance Brought by the Blood

3. The Blessings We May Obtain by the Blood

1. THE DANGER TO BE AVERTED BY THE BLOOD

The danger was awful: the eternal God was about to send the destroying angel with his sword through the land.

It was general: no house was to be spared. Each family was to be robbed of its crown: the firstborn must die.

It was certain: no power of man could procure redemption.

It was unexpected: a terrible picture of the danger that threatens us and from which there is no deliverance except by the blood of the Lamb.

That danger is awful. A hiding place, a means of redemption, has no value if danger is not realized. The blood of Jesus, however precious it is in the eyes of God and of the redeemed, has no value for him who has not realized his danger. The world is under the wrath of God. However happily life is spent, however we boast about our present civilization and prosperity and progress, there hangs over this world a heavy, dark cloud, more terrible than that which hung over Egypt. There is a day of judgment approaching, when anger and wrath, tribulation and anguish shall be recompensed to all disobedience and sin. Christ shall appear in flaming fire, taking vengeance on those who *"know not God, and that obey not the gospel"* (2 Thessalonians 1:8). He will pronounce that terrible sentence upon all who do not belong to Him: *"Depart from me, ye cursed, into everlasting fire, prepared for the devil and his angels"* (Matthew 25:41); *"Behold, the day cometh, that shall burn as an oven"; "and who shall stand when He appeareth?"* (Malachi 4:1, 3:2)

It is general. No house in Egypt was to be passed by. From the palace of the king to the hut of the beggar, the firstborn had to die. There was no distinction: rich and poor, godless and fashionable, friends and enemies of Israel, innocent children, those who were kind, as well as the cruelest oppressors of the people—that night there was no difference between them. The nation had sinned; the judgment must come upon all, without exception.

It will be just the same with the judgment that is coming upon the world. We all have sinned; we are all under a curse and wrath. No one—unless God Himself in a miraculous manner redeemed him—will escape a judgment that he cannot endure. No reader of these words, whoever he is, can escape standing before God's throne, to be cast into the outer darkness on account of his sins, if God's mercy has not wrought out for him a miracle of grace.

This judgment is certain. We are living in the days of which Scripture has spoken, when scoffers, walking after their own lusts, say: *"Where is the promise of his coming, for…all things continue as they were from the beginning of the creation"* (2 Peter 3:4). God is longsuffering and extends the days of grace, but the Day of Judgment will surely come. No power or force, no wisdom or cunning, no riches or honor can enable man to escape it. It comes certainly. As surely as there is a God in heaven who is a righteous judge, as surely as there is sin on earth opposed to God's holy law, as surely as there is in every child of man consciousness that sin must be punished by a judge, as surely, that day will come. Although the thought of the millions who then will be lost, of the terribleness of the breaking loose of the pent-up fire of God's wrath, and of the misery of an eternal destruction from God's presence is too terrible to rightly apprehend or bear—it is true and certain. There hangs over the whole world, and over every soul, a dark cloud of the wrath of God that will speedily break loose and burn with a fire that through eternity will not be extinguished.

The danger is unexpected. In Egypt they were busy buying and selling, building and trading, and living delicately and boasting about their power and wisdom, when in one night the whole land was plunged into the deepest sorrow. *"And Pharaoh rose up in the night, he, and all his servants, and all the Egyptians; and there was a great cry in Egypt"* (Exodus 12:30). It was in Egypt, as in the days of the flood, and of Sodom and Gomorrah; in an hour when they thought not, the angel of destruction came.

It will ever be so. The devil lulls men to sleep by the business and enjoyments of this world: Death comes—unexpected. Judgment comes—unexpected. While one still puts off to a more convenient season, while another comforts himself with the assurance that he will yet sometime be delivered, while still others do not trouble themselves at all about these things—judgment ever draws nearer. It has happened more than once that a man has fallen asleep on the railway line; everything around him seemed restful and still; suddenly the express train came rushing on and crushed him to death.

God's judgment draws near with incomprehensible rapidity and power. Because everything around you is quiet and safe and appears joyous, I beseech you, do not deceive yourselves. Judgment comes unexpectedly, and then—then it is forever too late. Believe this, I pray you, the danger is greater and nearer than you imagine; make haste to be delivered.

2. THE DELIVERANCE BROUGHT BY THE BLOOD

Deliverance is planned by God Himself. Let this be a settled conviction with you, that no human wisdom is of any avail here. It is from God's judgment, which is so terrible, that we must flee. It is God alone who can point out the way of escape. Deliverance by the blood of a lamb was the outcome of divine wisdom. If a sinner desires to be delivered, then he must learn in this matter to be entirely submissive to God and entirely dependent upon Him. He must see that he has to deal with what is really a divine purpose, and that, as sure and powerful as the destruction is, just so sure and powerful is the deliverance which has been prepared for him.

Deliverance is through substitution. That was the meaning of the blood of the slaughtered paschal lamb. The Israelite was just as sinful as the Egyptian. If the destroying angel came, he would have the right—yes (if we must go by right) it would be his duty to enter each house of Israel. But if on the door of the Israelite he found the blood—what does that mean?

When the Israelite took the lamb and raised the knife to slay that innocent creature for the sake of its blood, which he had need of for his deliverance, he had only one thought in his mind: "I am sinful; my house is sinful. The angel of God's wrath is coming tonight. If he acts according to what I deserve, then death would enter my house, but I offer this lamb to die for me and my house." That phrase "for me," "in my place," was the one thought in his heart. This lamb was typical: *"God will provide himself a lamb"* (Genesis 22:8). He has done this. He has—oh, wonder of wonders!—given His own Son to die in our place. The death that Jesus died was my death. He bore my sins. I need not now die. The deliverance that God has prepared is through substitution. Jesus, my substitute, has paid all—all my indebtedness to God's law—and has done everything for me. He has entirely broken the power of sin and death, and I can now, at once, be entirely acquitted and be freed from all my sins. Deliverance is through substitution. Deliverance is by means of the sprinkling of blood. The blood of the lamb had to be sprinkled on the door posts. It was not enough that the lamb should be slain and its bloodshed; the blood must be personally applied. The father of the family had to take the blood and sprinkle it on the door of his house. And so the Scripture says that our conscience must be cleansed and our heart must be sprinkled. *"Let us draw near...having our hearts sprinkled from an evil conscience"* (Hebrews 10:22).

Deliverance is through the obedience of faith. For the Israelite it was a new and hitherto unheard-of thing, that the destroying angel was to come, and that the blood on the door would deliver him. But he believed God's Word, and in that belief he did what he had been commanded. This is just what you have to do who are longing for deliverance from eternal death. Exercise faith in the blood. Be assured that if God tells you the blood of His Son cleanses you from all sin, that it is the truth. The blood has a supernatural, heavenly, divine power to cover and blot out sin before God immediately and forever. Accept this as God's truth and rest upon it. Then be obedient and appropriate that blood which accomplishes such wonders. Reckon that it was shed for you. Humble yourself before God, that the Holy Spirit may apply it to you and cleanse your heart by it. Simply believe in that blood as shed for you. The almighty God is faithful and will accept you for the sake of the blood. Jesus will cleanse you by His blood and will work out in you the cleansing and impart to you the joy and the power that the blood alone can bestow. The blood affects an immediate deliverance from the judgment of God. The blood delivered the Israelites immediately and entirely from the threatened danger of that night.

From the moment that you are sprinkled by that blood, you are justified from your sins, and the judgment of God is averted from you. This blessing is so great, so divine, that it appears to man too great to be true. We desire to see in ourselves some token of improvement, to feel something as a proof that God has received us. It seems incredible that God could thus justify the unrighteous immediately, and yet it is so. This is the divine glory of redemption through the blood of the Lamb. The blood has such a divine and life-giving power that the moment a man believes in it, he is cleansed from all his sins. You who desire to be saved from sin and judgment may rely upon this. The blood affects an immediate redemption. The blood is so unspeakably precious to God, as the proof of the obedience of His Son, that He, for Jesus' sake and because of His pleasure in Him, immediately forgives and receives you, if only you trust in that blood. The blood is the beginning of a new life. You know that the Feast of Unleavened Bread was closely connected with the Feast of the Passover. If leaven were used, it came from a portion of the old lump of dough of a previous baking. Leavening is a process of corruption. Israel had to use unleavened bread during the Passover Feast and the seven following days as a proof that they would no longer have anything to do with the old leaven of Egypt; everything must become entirely new. The sprinkling with the blood of Christ is the commencement of an entirely new life. The blood and the Spirit of Christ are inseparable. When the sinner is brought near to God by the blood, he is renewed and sanctified by the Spirit. The blood is the beginning and pledge of a life in the service of God.

The blood gave assurance of the love and guidance of God. Israel was delivered by the sprinkling of the blood from the power of the destroying angel and also from the power of Pharaoh. The Red Sea, the pursuit by Pharaoh, and the desert, were still to come, but the blood was the pledge that God would be responsible for everything.

The blood of Christ gives you a share in the love, the guidance, and the protection of God. Oh, if you only understood this—the God who has provided the blood of His Son, who has received you because of that blood—He has become your God. He who has given His Son for you, how shall He not with Him also freely give you all things? This is the blessing and power of the blood—it brings your into an eternal covenant with God; He becomes your leader and your portion.

3. THE BLESSINGS WE MAY OBTAIN BY THE BLOOD

When the Israelite had sprinkled the blood he knew that he was safe. God had given him a promise of protection, and he was able trustfully to await the terrible visit of the destroying angel. He could listen peacefully to the great cry in the streets around him. His safety lay in God, who had said: *"When I see the blood, I will pass over you"* (Exodus 12:13). How much more may we, who now have not the blood of an earthly lamb but that of the Lamb of God from heaven—how much more may we be assured of our redemption? You who read this, give, I pray you, an answer to the question I now ask: Have you this assurance? Are you truly sheltered from the day of wrath, under the protection of the blood? Have you the assurance that you also have been redeemed by that blood? If not, hasten, without delay, to receive this blessing. The danger is so terrible—the redemption is so glorious. The conditions are so full of grace. Let nothing keep you back from obtaining a share in it. You must be sure about it, or you will have no rest for your soul.

It is recorded that on the Passover night, there was an old grey-haired man who lived in the house of his firstborn son, and he himself was the firstborn son of his father. His son also had a firstborn son.

Thus, there were three firstborn sons in the house who all must die if the destroying angel entered the house. The old man was lying on his bed sick, but he heard with interest everything his son told him about God's command to Moses. Towards evening he was often restless, as he thought of their danger, and he said: "My son, are you sure that you have done everything that has been prescribed?" His answer was: "Yes, father, everything." For a moment he was satisfied. Then he asked again: "Are you sure? Has the blood been sprinkled on the door?" Again the answer was: "Yes, father, everything has been done according to the command." The nearer it came to midnight, the more restless he became. Finally, he cried out: "My son, carry me out if you please, that I may see it myself, and then I can rest." The son took his father up and carried him to where he could see the blood on the side posts and the lintel. "Now I am satisfied," he cried. "Thank God! Now I know that I am safe!"

My reader, can you say that—"Thank God, now I know that I am safe. I know that the blood was shed for me and has been sprinkled on me"? If not, I beseech you, by the terror and certainty of the judgment of God, make haste this day to hearken to God's Word. Turn away from your sin and place your trust in the blood. Oh! I pray you, add not now to all your other sins that of despising, rejecting, treading upon the blood of the Son of God. I beseech you by the mercy of God, and the wondrous love of the Son of God, flee from the wrath to come and seek for shelter under the blood that alone can redeem. Believe, I beseech you, that no prayer, no worship, no works, no endeavor, will avail you anything. But God has said: *"When I see the blood, I will pass over you"* (Exodus 12:13). Let that be your confidence. If He does see the blood on me, He will spare me. Come now, today, to this dear Savior, who lives to cleanse you with His blood, and who never once has rejected anyone who came to Him.

8
PURCHASED BY THE BLOOD

Thou art worthy…for thou wast slain,
and hast redeemed us to God by thy blood.
—Revelation 5:9

Bought: that word is understood by everybody. Trading occupies a great place in our lives. We are all so constantly engaged in buying or selling that the ideas attached to it are understood by everybody. The right that the buyer obtains over that which previously had not been his; the value that he attaches to it after its price has been paid; the certainty that what he has bought will be given to him; and the use that he will make of his purchase; all these things are obvious. Daily, in a thousand ways, they make out the life of the community. The words of our text, taken from a heavenly hymn of praise: *"Thou…hast redeemed us to God by thy blood,"* invite us to see in the mirror of earthly trade what *"the blood of the Lamb"* (Revelation 12:11) has done for us and what a clear knowledge of this fact entails. The right to us that our Lord Jesus, *"the Lamb of God"* (John 1:29), has obtained, and the claim that we now have in regard to Him, what we may expect from Him, what He expects from us—all these things will become plain to us. If the Holy Spirit teaches us to regard the blood in the light of these resemblances, our hearts surely will take up the song of heaven with new joy: *"Thou art worthy…for thou wast slain, and hast redeemed us to God by thy blood"* (Revelation 5:9).

Following these thoughts let us notice:

1. The Right to Us, which He Has Obtained

2. The Claim He Makes upon Us

3. The Joy with which He Will Receive Us

4. The Certainty that He Will Protect and Care for Us

1. THE RIGHT TO US, WHICH HE HAS OBTAINED

"*Thou...hast redeemed us to God by thy blood*," that indicates the right to us that He has obtained. As Creator, the Lord Jesus has a right to every soul of man. Through Him, God has bestowed life upon men, that they might be His possession and inheritance. Never on earth has any maker had such a right over his own work as Jesus has over us; we belong to Him. "It has often happened among men that one has had to buy back what really belonged to him but had been taken from him by a hostile power. Many times a person has had to buy back their land and freedom by their blood. After that, land and liberty become of increased value." Thus, the Son of God has ransomed us from the power of Satan. God, at creation, had placed man under the government of His Son. By yielding to the temptations of Satan, man fell from God and became entirely subject to the authority of the tempter; he became his slave. It was the law of God that prohibited sin and threatened punishment. When man sinned, it was this law that bestowed upon Satan his authority. God has said: "*In the day that thou eatest*" (Genesis 2:17), thou fallest into the power of death. God Himself gave man up to be a slave in the prison house of Satan. For man there was no possibility of redemption except by ransom—by the payment of the price that the law must righteously demand as ransom for the redemption of prisoners.

You know that word "redemption." In old times when it was the custom that prisoners of war were made slaves, sometimes a very high price was paid by the friends or rulers of the prisoners as ransom for their deliverance from slavery. Jesus Christ has purchased, with His own blood, our freedom from the prison and slavery of Satan. It is that prison in which he, as our enemy, had lodged us and to which the law of God had condemned us. To purchase, to ransom, means always that one valuable thing is given for another. Our souls needed redemption: the law demanded the payment of a ransom. We were under its power and condemnation. We were held as prisoners until what we owed was paid, a recompense for the wrongs we had done—a perfect righteousness. Jesus came and gave Himself in our place: His soul for our soul. He bore our punishment of death, our curse of death. He shed His blood as reconciliation for our sin. That blood was the ransom price by which we are redeemed. He gave His life for our life. His blood gave Him an eternal right to us. And now the message comes to us as from heaven—Jesus has bought us by His blood. He, and none else, has a right to us. Not Satan, not the world, and not ourselves have any right to us. The Son of God has bought us with His blood. He alone has a right to us; we belong to Him.

2. THE CLAIM HE MAKES UPON US

"*Thou…hast redeemed us to God by thy blood*" (Revelation 5:9). These words remind us of the claim that He makes on us. A person may have a right to something without exercising that right; he lays no claim to it. But it is not thus with Jesus Christ. He comes to us with the urgent request that we should surrender ourselves to Him. You know how, in every ordinary purchase, the buyer has the right to ask that what he has purchased shall be given to him. It is carefully stated when and where the delivery will take place. Jesus Christ sends His servants with the request that without delay—that at the hour and in the place where the message is delivered—there the persons, as His purchased possession, should hand themselves over and become subject to Him. That message comes to you again today. He entreats you to say farewell to all foreign authority that has ruled over you and to become His sole possession.

Chief among those foreign powers is sin. By our descent from fallen Adam, sin has a terrible authority over us. It has soaked to the deepest roots of our nature; it is thoroughly at home in us; it has become our nature. However strongly we may be inclined to forsake sin—whether by the voice of God, our own conscience, or some desire to do good—sin refuses to release us. As slaves of sin, we have no power to break the bonds that bind us. But Jesus, who has bought us by His blood, now calls upon us to give ourselves to Him. However deeply we experience that we have been sold under sin and that the law of sin always holds us prisoners, He promises to deliver us from its tyranny. He promises that He will Himself bestow upon us the power to serve and follow Him as Lord. He asks only for the choice of our hearts, the honest declaration of our will, that we recognize His right and yield ourselves to Him. He will see to it that the authority of sin shall be destroyed.

Another of the foreign powers that has exercised authority over us is the world. The needs and business of the world are so manifold and so urgent, they lay claim to our lives and all our powers. The promises, the enjoyments, the temptations which the world presents to us are so flattering, and exercise such an unconscious influence upon us, that it is impossible for us of ourselves to offer resistance to them. The favor and assistance of the people we associate with, their displeasure and contempt if we separate ourselves from them to live only for God, work out in many an enslavement to the world. It rules over them and demands their obedience. Satan is the ruler of this world and through it exercises his power over them. Jesus Christ comes as Conqueror of Satan and the world and asks us to choose which we wish to serve—Him, or this enemy of His. He asks this of us, as those who belong to Him. He points us to His blood, to the right to us that He has obtained, and asks that we should recognize this right and surrender ourselves as His possession.

There is another power, a still stronger one, foreign and hostile to Christ. It is the power of self. It is here that sin has wrought its most terrible ruin. The doing of our own will, seeking our own pleasure and our own honor, are so deeply rooted in us that apart from an entire revolution it can never be otherwise. Body and soul, understanding and imagination, inclination and love—all are subject to the terrible power of self-pleasing, to the tyranny of self. Jesus Christ asks that self should be pulled down from the throne and condemned to death. He asks that in all things His will and not ours should be supreme. He beseeches us to make an end of slavery to other lords and to give ourselves up to Him as His purchased possession. Each of us must deal with this claim, this request of *"the Lamb of God."* How you deal with it will decide what your life will be in time and in eternity. A voice comes to us from heaven, saying: "He is worthy; He has been slain; He has purchased us to God by His blood" (see Revelation 5:9). Oh, that our hearts might no longer hesitate, but by faith in that divine blood respond to His call and reply: "Thou art worthy, O Lord! Here I am, take what Thou hast purchased. I yield myself to Thee as Thy possession."

3. THE JOY WITH WHICH HE WILL RECEIVE US

"Thou…hast redeemed us to God by thy blood"—that gives us the pledge of the joy with which He will receive us. When a sinner has been urged to give himself to the Lord, and he declares his willingness to do so, he is, alas, often hindered by the fear that he is unworthy to be received. He feels himself so sinful, so dead. He feels he is so greatly lacking in humility and real earnestness, and in that heartfelt love that befits one who desires to give himself to such a Lord, that he cannot believe the Lord will receive him so instantly, so fully and so eternally. He cannot understand it, still less does he feel in his heart that it is true. What a glorious answer to all these questionings is in this word, *"Thou…hast redeemed us to God by thy blood."* Do you not know that if a person buys anything he will surely take possession of it if it is brought to him? You have, I suppose, sometime bought something? As you have paid your money for it and it was given or brought to you were you not willing to receive it and take possession of it? The higher the price you paid for it, the less was there any doubt that you would take possession of what you had paid for. "But"—you will perhaps answer—"if I buy something, I know what it is, and that it is worth the price I paid. But I, with my sinful heart, with everything so dead and miserable—there is reason for me to fear that He who purchased me will not receive me. I am not what I ought to be. When I buy an article and another of less

worth is sent to me, I refuse to receive it. I send it back with the message: 'This is not what I bought and for which I have paid.'"

You are right, but consider what the difference is between Him who has bought us by His blood and human purchasers. He bought what He knew was bad, *because* it was bad, and which He will *accept* as bad, that His love may have the joy and glory of making it good. How wonderful this It is nevertheless true; the worse you are, and the deeper you have sunk in the helplessness of your sin, the more fit you are for Him. The Scripture says: *"Christ died for the ungodly...while we were yet sinners, Christ died for us"* (Romans 5:6, 8). It says, further, that the price of Christ's blood was paid for those who denied the Lord, for those who sold Him, even for His rejecters. Understand, I pray you, that Jesus has paid an eternal price for you, as one who is an enemy, as one who is a lawful slave of Satan, as one entirely dead in sin. He comes to you who are in this condition with the request that you will surrender yourself to Him, and with a promise that He will receive you just as you are.

4. THE CERTAINTY THAT HE WILL PROTECT AND CARE FOR US

"Thou...hast redeemed us to God by thy blood." This assures us that He will preserve us and care for us. The man who has purchased something of value, for instance a good horse, not only receives it when it is brought to him, but he appreciates it, he takes care of it, and provides for it. He exercises it and he uses it. He does all this that he may have the utmost service and pleasure out of it. When Jesus Christ receives us— however glorious that is—it is only the beginning. We can rely on Him who bought us by His blood to complete His work in us. It is just the want of insight into this truth that holds many troubled persons back from surrender and causes many of weak faith to live always in trouble and worry. They do not apply to spiritual things what they understand so well in earthly affairs. When a man has paid a high price for something, even if only a horse or a sheep, he takes it for granted that he must

care for it so that he may have pleasure and service from it. And the Lord Jesus—how is it that you do not understand it?—takes it upon Himself to care for you, and so to order things that He may attain His purpose in you. You cannot guard yourself against temptation or going astray. You cannot manage yourself or make yourself fit for His service. You cannot direct yourself so that you may know how to act in everything according to His will and that of the Father. You cannot do it. But He can; He will, as the One who has bought you with His blood.

My fellow believer, the right that the Lord Jesus has obtained to you is so infinitely high, so broad, so unlimited, that if you will only think about it, you will respond to it. Just as I desire that every member of my body—the eye, the ear, the hand, the foot—should always be at my service, so the Lord desires that you, as a member of His body, along with every power and faculty, should always without a moment's break serve Him. You are so far from being able to do this that you do not even apprehend it. Cease trying to do it, and begin each day by committing yourself to the almighty preservation and control of your Lord. Just as a horse or a sheep with each new day must be cared for afresh by its owner, even more so must you, as the property of the Son of God, be cared for by Him. Christ is not an owner who is outside of you, or who is only in heaven above; He is your Head. And just as the first Adam lives within you with his sinful nature, so He, as the second Adam, lives in you with His holy nature and by His Holy Spirit. And the one thing to which He calls you is to trust Him, to wait on Him, to rely confidently upon Him to finish in the outward things of our lives His hidden and unnoticed work of protection and perfection. Would that each one of us might know what is implied by our being accepted as the blood-bought possession of Jesus.

It implies that He has set a very high value upon us, and so He will not allow any evil to befall us. He will manifest His love to us. He has need of us for His work and glory, and it is His desire and joy to adorn us with His salvation and to fill us with His unspeakable joy. Meditate upon this till it becomes fixed firmly in your mind. It implies that our great need is to recognize ourselves as His possession and, by a reverent confession of this, to have our hearts filled by the consciousness of it. Just as a faithful dog often shows so great an attachment to his owner that he will not cease following him, let the wonderful ownership of Jesus, His blood-bought right, so possess you that it will every moment be the keynote of your life and the power of an enduring attachment to Him.

Also, it implies that we should cultivate trust in Him, and let it completely control our whole soul and every thought as to how we are to spend our life and do our work. A possession is preserved and cared for by the owner. Jesus is my heavenly and almighty Owner, who has bought me for Himself by His blood and prizes me as "the dear purchase" of that blood. He will surely protect me, He will surely make me fit for all things in which He intends to make use of me.

"Thou art worthy...for thou wast slain, and hast redeemed us to God by thy blood." Oh, my readers, listen, I pray you, to the song of heaven, and let it begin to sound in your heart. Let it be the heart confession of your relationship to the slain Lamb. Remember that the blood is the power that binds us to Jesus in bonds that cannot be loosened. Let him who has not yet acknowledged the claim of Christ do so today, and let him now say: "Thou art worthy; for the sake of Thy blood Thou shalt have me."

Let him who has already acknowledged the Lord's claim abandon himself to the heavenly influences of the Holy Spirit for the destruction of all doubt and slowness of heart and for the enduement of power to live wholly for the Lamb of God.

Meditate upon and adore God for this divine wonder, that you have been bought by the blood of the Son of God. Let your life become a testimony of the song: *"Thou art worthy...for thou wast slain, and hast redeemed us to God by thy blood."*

9

THE BLOOD AND THE TRINITY

Peter...to the...elect according to the foreknowledge of God the Father,
through sanctification of the Spirit, unto obedience and the sprinkling
of the blood of Jesus Christ: Grace unto you,
and peace, be multiplied.
—1 Peter 1:1–2

The tri-unity of the Godhead is often considered as merely a matter of doctrine and having no close relationship to the Christian life.

This is not the view of the New Testament when it describes the work of redemption or the idea of the life of God. In the epistles the three Persons are constantly named together, so that in each activity of grace all three together have a share in it. God is triune; but in everything that He does, and at all times, the Three are One.

This is in entire agreement with what we see in nature. A trinity is found in everything. There is the hidden, inner nature, the outward form, and the effect. It is not otherwise in the Godhead. The Father is the eternal being—I AM—the hidden foundation of all things and fountain of all life. The Son is the outward form, the express image, the revelation of God. The Spirit is the executive power of the Godhead. The nature of the hidden unity is revealed and made known in the Son, and it is imparted to us and is experienced by us through the agency of the Spirit. In all their activities the Three are inseparably One.

Everything is *of* the Father; everything is *in* the Son; everything is *through* the Spirit.

In the words of our text that Peter writes to believers to whom also he sends his greetings, we find the relationship in which each redeemed one stands to the three Persons of the Godhead is clearly set forth.

They are elect *"according to the foreknowledge of God."* The source of our redemption is in the counsel of God.

They are chosen in *"sanctification of the Spirit"*: the entire carrying out of the counsel of God is through the Holy Spirit and the sanctification and the impartation of divine holiness which He works.

They are elect to *"obedience and the sprinkling of the blood of Jesus Christ."* The final purpose of God is the restoration of man to a state where the will of God will be done on earth as it is done in heaven. Then everything will reflect the glory of the free grace that has been revealed so gloriously in the death and blood of the Son of God.

The place that *"the sprinkling of blood"* takes is most remarkable. It is mentioned last, as the great final end in which, according to the foreknowledge of the Father, the sanctification of the Spirit, and the submission to the obedience of Christ, it finds completion.

In order that we may understand its place and worth in redemption, let us consider it in the light of:

1. The Glorious Purpose of the Triune God

2. The Mighty Power, by which that Purpose Was Attained

3. The Counsel in which Everything Originated

1. THE GLORIOUS PURPOSE OF THE TRIUNE GOD

Christians are described as *"elect unto...obedience and the sprinkling of the blood of Jesus Christ."* In the Holy Trinity the place occupied by the Lord Jesus is characterized by the name that He bore as "the only begotten Son of God." (See John 3:16.) He is literally and really the only One with whom God the Father can or will have anything to do. As the Son, He is the mediator through whom God worked in creation, and by whom the creature can draw near to God. God dwells in the hidden and unapproachable light of a consuming fire: Christ is the Light of lights, the Light in which we can view and enjoy the Deity. And the eternal election of God can have no higher purpose than to give us a share in Christ and, through Him, approach to the Father Himself.

What these blessings are is clearly revealed to us in the Word of God. *"Ye who were afar off have been made nigh by the blood of Christ"* (Ephesians 2:13). *"Having boldness to enter into the holiest through the blood of Jesus"* (Hebrews 10:19). "He has cleansed us from our sins by His blood" (see 1 John 1:7). *"How much more shall the blood of Christ… purge your conscience…to serve the living God"* (Hebrews 9:14). *"The blood of Jesus Christ…cleanses from all sin"* (1 John 1:7). Many such statements show us that the cleansing and fitness to draw near to God, that the true and living entrance into fellowship with Him, is the blessed effect of *"the sprinkling of blood"* on our heart and conscience. In the depths of eternity that blood of sprinkling was the object of the unspeakable good pleasure of the Father as the means of redemption of His elect. It is obvious that when that blood becomes the good pleasure and joy of a sinner, and he seeks life and salvation in that blood, then the heart of God and the heart of the sinner meet one another. It is there that an inner agreement and fellowship, which nothing can break, is found in the blood. The Father has elected us to the sprinkling of the blood, that we may heartily accept it and find our entire salvation in it.

There is still another word to consider: elect to obedience and the sprinkling of the blood of Jesus Christ. Here the two sides of the life of grace are placed together for us in a most striking way. In *"the sprinkling of the blood"* we learn what Christ has done *for* and *to* us. In *"obedience"* we have what is expected *from* us. The creature can have no other blessedness than that found in the will of God, and in doing it as it is done in heaven. The fall was simply the turning away of man from God's will to do his own will. Jesus came to alter this and to bring us again into obedience. And God lets us know that He, in His eternal choice, had these two things in view: *"obedience"* and *"the sprinkling of the blood."*

The placing together of these two words teaches us the very important lesson that obedience and the *"sprinkling of the blood"* are inseparably united. It was so with the Lord Jesus. Apart from His obedience, the shedding of His blood would have been of no value. The blood is the life. That life consists of inner nature and will. The power of Jesus' blood lies wholly in this, that He offered Himself without spot to God, to do His will, subjecting His own will utterly to the will of God. *"He… became obedient unto death…*[therefore] *God also hath highly exalted him"* (Philippians 2:8–9). He who receives the blood of Jesus receives with it, as his life, His inner nature of utter obedience to God. *"Obedience"* and *"the sprinkling of the blood"* are inseparably bound together. The inner nature manifested by Christ in the shedding of His blood must become the nature of those on whom it has been sprinkled.

If any Christian asks why he enjoys so little of the peace and cleansing of the blood, he may be almost certain that the reason is that he has not fully surrendered himself to be obedient. If anyone asks how he may obtain the full enjoyment of the power of the blood—the reply may be: "Set yourself resolutely to obey God. Let your motto be: 'My will in nothing—God's will in everything'; that is what the blood of your Redeemer teaches you." Do not separate what God from the beginning has joined together—obedience and the sprinkling of the blood—and you will thus be led into the fullness of blessing. From eternity God has elected you to both obedience and the sprinkling of the blood.

2. THE MIGHTY POWER, BY WHICH THAT PURPOSE WAS ATTAINED

The Holy Spirit is the great power of God. In the Holy Trinity He proceeds from the Father and the Son. He, by His omnipotent but hidden activity, executes the divine purpose. He reveals and makes known the Father and the Son. In the New Testament the word holy is applied to Him more often than to the Father or the Son. He is almost always called the Holy Spirit because it is He who from the inward being of God transfers holiness to the redeemed. The life of God is where His holiness dwells. Where the Holy Spirit imparts the life of God, there He imparts and maintains the holiness of God, and thus is called the Spirit of sanctification. So the text says that we are *"elect…through the sanctification of the Spirit, unto obedience and the sprinkling of the blood of Christ"* (1 Peter 1:2). It is committed to the Holy Spirit by His holy power to watch over us and to fulfill God's purpose in us. We are elect in sanctification of the Spirit unto obedience.

The Spirit of sanctification and obedience: these two go together in the purpose of God. Here we have also a solution to the difficulty already mentioned, that it is not possible for us to render the obedience that God demands. Because God knew this much better than we do, He has made provision for it. He bestows upon us the Spirit of sanctification, who so renews our heart and inward nature and fills us with His holy and heavenly power that it becomes really possible for us to be obedient. The one needful thing is that we should recognize and trust in the indwelling of the Holy Spirit and follow His leading.

His inward activity is so gentle and hidden, He unites Himself so entirely with us and our endeavors, that we still imagine that it is our own thinking or willing, where He has already been the hidden worker. Through this disregard of Him, we cannot believe that when we have a conviction of sin, or a willingness to obey (both the result of His inward activity), that He has also power to perfect that work in us. Let him, therefore, who really desires to be obedient, be persistently and quietly careful to maintain this attitude of trustful confidence: *"The Spirit of the Lord is upon me"* (Luke 4:18). Let him bow reverently before God with the prayer that He would be *"strengthened with might by his Spirit in the inner man"* (Ephesians 3:16).

In sanctification of the Spirit: this supplies the power that enables us to be obedient, and through which also we experience what the sprinkling of the blood means and imparts. This is the reason why so many of God's people have to complain that after all they have learned and heard and thought and believed about the blood, they experience so little of its power. This is not to be wondered at, for that learning and hearing and thinking and believing is in a great part only a work of the understanding. And even when prayer is made for the Holy Spirit, it is all in expectation that He will give us clearer *ideas* of the truth. No—this is not the way. The Spirit dwells in the heart: it is there He desires to do His first and greatest work. The heart must first be made right, and then the understanding will lay hold of the truth, not merely as a mental idea, but as an inner strength for the Christian life. We are chosen in sanctification of the Spirit—not in the activities of the understanding—to the sprinkling of the blood.

Everyone who desires to know the power of the blood of Jesus must remember that the Spirit and the blood bear witness together. It was by the shedding of the blood, and by the sprinkling of that blood before God in heaven, that the Spirit was free to come and dwell among us and in us. It was to assure the hearts of the disciples concerning the glorious result of the blood in heaven, in opening a free and bold entrance to God, and to make them partakers of the blessedness and power of the heavenly life that was now their portion, that the Holy Spirit was sent into their hearts. The first Pentecost, in all its power and blessing, is our portion also, our inheritance. Would that we might cease to seek in our own strength the salvation and blessings purchased for us by the blood.

We have seen what is the work of the Son and of the Spirit; let us now ascend to see the place that the Father occupies.

3. THE COUNSEL IN WHICH EVERYTHING ORIGINATED

Peter writes to the *"elect according to the foreknowledge of God the Father, through sanctification of the Spirit, unto obedience and the sprinkling of the blood of Jesus Christ"* (1 Peter 1:2). The counsel of the Father is the origin of everything, and that is in the Godhead as well as in the work of redemption. In the Godhead, the Son proceeds from the Father, and the Spirit proceeds from the Father and the Son. The whole counsel of redemption is also solely *"according to the purpose of him who worketh all things after the counsel of his own will"* (Ephesians 1:11). From the greatest—the ordering of the work of the Son and of the Holy Spirit—to the least—the day to day occurrences in His kingdom—all this is the work of the Father. Sanctification of the Spirit, obedience, and the sprinkling of the blood are the portion of the elect, according to the foreknowledge of the Father.

You may, with the most entire confidence, reckon that He who has thought out this wonderful counsel so far, and gloriously carried it out in the sprinkling of the blood and the sending of the Spirit, will just as surely and gloriously carry it out in your soul. This is the right use of the doctrine of predestination—leading you to cast yourself down before God and to acknowledge that from Him, and through Him, and to Him are all things, and to expect everything from Him alone. Take your place before God, my fellow believer, in deep reverence and complete dependence. Do not imagine that now that God has revealed Himself in Christ and by the Spirit, which you, by making use of what you have learned from this revelation, can work out your own salvation. Let it not be thought of! God must work in you to will and to do before you can work it out. God must work in you by the Spirit, and by Him must reveal Christ in you. Give God the glory, and let the fullest dependence upon Him be the keynote of your life of faith. If God does not do everything in you, all is in vain. If you expect anything from yourself, you will receive nothing; if you expect all from God, God will do everything in you. Let your expectation be from God alone. Apply this to all upon which we have been meditating concerning obedience.

Apply it especially to the blessed *"sprinkling of the blood"* of Jesus Christ. It was this that led us to the choice of this text. Your heart is longing with great desire—is it not?—to live every day under the clear consciousness: "I have been sprinkled with the eternal, precious, divine blood of the Lamb." Your heart longs after all the blessed effects of that blood—redemption, pardon, peace, cleansing, sanctification, drawing near to God, joy, and victory—all of which come through the blood. Your heart longs to experience constantly these blessings in full measure. Cast fear aside—you have been elected by God to the sprinkling of the blood of Christ Jesus. You must steadfastly rely on the fact that God, as God, will bestow it upon you. Wait continually upon Him in patience of soul, and confidently expect it. He *"who worketh all things after to the counsel of his own will"* (Ephesians 1:11); He Himself will surely work it out in you.

Apply this also to the sanctification of the Spirit. He is the link that binds together the middle and the end. His is the power that brings together the eternal purpose of God and a life of obedience and the sprinkling of the blood. Do you feel that this is the one thing that you desire and for which you must wait that you may inherit the full blessing? Understand that it is God Himself who bestows the Spirit, who works through the Spirit, who will fill you by the Spirit. How can God who elected you *"in sanctification of the Spirit"* (1 Peter 1:2) allow you to lack that without which His purpose cannot be carried out? Be confident about this; ask and expect it with utter boldness. It is possible to live in the sanctification of the Spirit because it has been designed for you from eternity.

The sprinkling of the blood is the light or revelation of the Trinity—how wonderful and glorious it is! The Father designed the sprinkling of the blood and elected us to it. The Son shed His blood and bestows it on the obedient from heaven. The Spirit of sanctification makes it our own, with abiding power, and imparts to us all the blessings that He has obtained for us. Blessed sprinkling of the blood! Revelation of the triune God! May this be our joy and our life each day.

10

WASHED IN HIS BLOOD

*Unto him that loved us, and washed us from our sins in his own blood,
and has made us kings and priests unto God and his Father; to him be
glory and dominion forever and ever. Amen.*
—Revelation 1:5–6

The apostle John dwelt in spirit before the doors of an open heaven when he was in Patmos. Time after time he saw in divine visions the glory of God and of the Lamb and of the redeemed. Of all the things that he saw, the most wonderful was that which caused the four living creatures, the four and twenty elders, the angels, the redeemed, and the whole creation to fall down repeatedly in ecstasy and adoration—the vision of the Lamb standing as it had been slain, in the midst of the throne. And of everything that he heard, that which most deeply impressed him was the frequent mention made in heaven of the blood of the Lamb. In the hymn of praise of the redeemed he had heard the words: *"Thou art worthy...for thou wast slain, and hast redeemed us to God by thy blood"* (Revelation 5:9). And in the reply of the elder to the question to which John could give no answer, he offered this explanation: *"These are they which...have washed their robes, and made them white in the blood of the Lamb"* (Revelation 7:14). John had been commanded to describe what he had seen and heard. He commences his book by a greeting similar to those we find in the epistles—*"Grace be unto you, and peace, from him which is, and which was, and which is to come"* (Revelation 1:4)—the eternal God. Then he mentions the Spirit: *"and from the seven Spirits which are before his throne"* (verse 4); and then follow these words: *"and from Jesus Christ"* (verse 5)—as he had seen Him—*"the first begotten of the dead, and the prince of the kings of the earth"* (verse 5).

The mention of the name of the Lord filled John's heart with joy and praise. Impressed by what he had heard in heaven, he cried out: *"Unto him that loved us, and washed us from our sins in his own blood, and hath made us kings and priests...to him be the glory and dominion for ever and ever. Amen"* (verses 5–6).

It is the blood, and being washed in that blood, which is the central point in his praise. The blessing seemed truly glorious and heavenly to John. He saw that blood linked with the love and salvation Christ has given us. And his heart, set on fire with a heavenly zeal, cried out, *"To him be glory and dominion for ever and ever"* (1 Peter 5:11). We have for some time been meditating upon the blood of Jesus. If there is one thing that befits us, which would be a proof that we have recognized something of the glory and power of that blood, it would be that we also, as we think of it, cry out: *"To him be glory... for ever and ever."* We shall consider John's song of praise. May it be granted to us to see something of what he saw, to feel something of what he felt, to receive something of the fire that inspired him, and to bring something of the offering of praise that he brought. Let us to that end fix our attention on the place which the blood occupies in this thanksgiving and inquire what it means that:

1. He Has Washed Us in His Blood

2. He Has Made Us Kings and Priests

3. He Loved Us

4. To Him be the Glory and Power for Ever and Ever

1. HE HAS WASHED US IN HIS BLOOD

We know what the word "washing" means. We wash our bodies to cleanse them from the least defilement that adheres to us. Our clothes are washed to remove every stain or spot. Now, sin is not merely a transgression of the law of God that is reckoned to us as guilt from which we must obtain acquittal or pardon. Sin has an effect upon our souls. It is a pollution that cleaves to us. The blood of Jesus procures for us more than the pardon for our guilt. When this has been powerfully brought to our hearts by the Holy Spirit—then at the same time the blood manifests the full deliverance of its cleansing power so that our souls know that they have been washed whiter than snow.

John speaks of this two-fold work of grace in his first epistle. He writes: *"If we confess our sins, he is faithful and just to forgive us our sins, and to cleanse us from all unrighteousness"* (1 John 1:9). To the same effect he had previously said: *"If we walk in the light, as he is in the light"*—that is in the pardoning and sanctifying love of God—*"we have fellowship one with another, and the blood of Jesus Christ his Son cleanseth us from all sin"* (verse 7). This refers to the abiding and uninterrupted cleansing of sin in the case of him who walks in the light, in fellowship with God.

Where does this washing take place, and what is it really that is washed? It is the heart. It is in the deep, hidden, inner life of man that this effect of the blood is experienced. Jesus said, *"the kingdom of God is within you"* (Luke 17:21). Sin has penetrated into the heart, and the whole nature has become saturated with it. The blood too must penetrate the heart; as deeply as the power of sin has gone, so deeply must the inner being be cleansed by the blood. We know that when some article of clothing is washed, the water with its cleansing power must soak in as deeply as the stain, if it is to be removed. Even so must the blood of Jesus penetrate to the deepest roots of our being. Our heart and our entire personality must be reached by the cleansing power of the blood. "The blood cleanses from all sin." (See 1 John 1:7.) Where sin has reached, there too must the blood follow it; where sin ruled, there the blood must rule. The entire heart must be cleansed by the blood. However great may be the depth of the heart, however manifold and lively its activities may be, the blood is just as wonderful and penetrating in its effects. It is in our hearts that the cleansing by the blood of Jesus must take place.

We are told: *"They…have washed their robes, and made them white in the blood of the Lamb"* (Revelation 7:14).

A person's position or character can often be told by his clothing. Royal robes are a sign of royal estate. Filthy or torn garments are a sign of poverty or carelessness. "White robes" indicate a holy character. Thus we read of the Lamb's Bride, *"To her was granted that she should be arrayed in fine linen, clean and white: for the fine linen is the righteousness of saints"* (Revelation 19:8). (*"Righteousness"* here is the translation of a word that means "the righteous acts.")

The message of the Lord Jesus to the church at Sardis was: *"Thou hast a few names even in Sardis which have not defiled their garments; and they shall walk with me in white: for they are worthy"* (Revelation 3:4).

Out of the heart *"are the issues of life"* (Proverbs 4:23)—just in proportion as the heart is cleansed, so the entire life is cleansed, the whole man inwardly and outwardly is cleansed by the power of the blood.

How is this washing effected? It is done by our Lord Jesus Himself who *"washed us from our sins in his own blood"* (Revelation 1:5). The washing began in an act personally accomplished in us by our Lord. He alone can perfect the work that He carries on in us by the Holy Spirit. Sin invaded our lives. Our powers of thought, will, and feeling were all brought under its authority. This was not an authority exercised from without, or occasionally, but one that was so united with these powers of ours that they themselves became altogether sinful. But now the Holy Spirit takes possession of the place in which sin had become entrenched. *"The Spirit is life"* (Romans 8:10), and He becomes the life of our lives. Through Him the Lord Jesus carries on His work in us. Through Him also the blood is constantly applied in its cleansing power. Our Lord is a High Priest in *"the power of an endless life"* (Hebrews 7:16), and thus the cleansing power of the blood of the Son of God is unceasingly conveyed to us. As we wash and cleanse ourselves daily, and thus are refreshed and invigorated, so the Lord bestows upon the soul that trusts in Him the enjoyment of a constant sense of cleansing by the blood. It is He Himself who cleanses us from sin, while we on our part receive the cleansing by faith, by that faith through which at first we receive the pardon of sin. But faith's capacity is now enlarged by obtaining a spiritual view of the divine power and continuous activity of the blood. By this insight, faith obtains a spiritual understanding and becomes able to apprehend the fact that just as the blood has had an infinite effect in the holiest in heaven, so sin has been completely and finally atoned for before God. Faith beholds the Lord Jesus, the great High Priest, living in the heart. He cleanses it in the blood that ever retains its power. Faith has learned that full salvation consists in one thing—Jesus Himself who has cleansed us by His blood is our *life*.

2. HE HAS MADE US KINGS AND PRIESTS

This is the position for which we are prepared and to which we are exalted by the cleansing of the blood. In this the power of the blood is manifested. If we wish to fully comprehend the spiritual connection between these two positions that are ours through the blood, we must learn it from the experience of the Lord Jesus Himself.

It was only after He had shed His blood that He was able to enter the holiest as Priest and to ascend the throne as King. It was His blood that conquered sin, and by it He was consecrated to enter into the holiest, into God's presence as Priest. The blood bestowed on Him the right, as Victor, to rule as King in the glory of God. Such is the heavenly and divine power that the blood possesses.

Now, when the blood comes into contact with us, and we by faith recognize its full power, it produces in us also the nature and fitness to become priests and kings. As long as we think that forgiveness of sins is all that is to be obtained by the blood, we shall neither understand what the kingly priesthood means, nor shall we have any desire for it. But when the Holy Spirit teaches and enables us to believe that the blood can accomplish in us also what it accomplished in the Lord Jesus personally, then the heart is opened to receive this glorious truth. The blood opens the way into a kingly priesthood. It was so to the Lord Jesus, it may be so with us also.

What now does it mean that He, when He has cleansed us by His blood, also makes us priests and kings to God and His Father? The principal idea attached to the title "king" is that of authority and rule, to the title "priest" that of purity and nearness to God. The blood of Jesus constitutes us priests and gives us admission into the presence, the love, and the fellowship of God. We are so cleansed by the blood as to be prepared for this. Jesus so fills us with His Spirit, with Himself, that we in Him may truly draw near to God as priests. The blood of Jesus carries in it so much of His victory over sin and death that it inspires us with the consciousness of His victorious power and bestows upon us victory over sin and every enemy. He makes us kings. Jesus, the living, priestly King on the throne, cannot manifest in us His full power by exercising it from above, or from the outside, but only by indwelling. When He, the priestly King, takes up His abode within us, He makes us kings and priests.

Do we wish to know the purpose of this? The answer is not far to seek. Why is Jesus seated as a priest on the throne of the heavens? It is that man may be blessed, and that God may be glorified in man. As priest He lives only for others, to bring them near to God. He lives as King only that He might reveal the kingdom of God in us and through us. He makes us priests that we might serve the living God, that we might bring others near to Him, that we might be filled with his Spirit so as to be a blessing to others.

3. HE LOVED US

We have spoken of the blood in which Jesus has cleansed us and of the glory to which He has exalted us. Let us now ascend to the fountain-head from which all this flows out to us—it is that He loved us. If we desire really to understand the salvation that God bestows upon us—to understand it so that it will tune our voices to sing like that of John, *"unto him be glory"* (Ephesians 3:21)—we must first of all understand that its origin and power are in the love of Jesus. Love is the greatest glory of salvation. As it springs from love as its source, it must lead us to that love as its object and nature. Love always suggests a personal, mutual attachment. This is the most wonderful thing in salvation, and it is almost impossible to fully comprehend—that the Lord Jesus desires to honor us with His love and His friendship. He wishes to have fellowship with us as His loved ones and to fill and satisfy our hearts with His divine love.

It is John especially who teaches us what this love is. In his gospel he tells us the Lord Jesus Christ said that as the Father loved Him, so He also loved us. Our Lord was one with the Father in nature and life. It is difficult for us to form any idea of what that unity is. But love, as the revelation of this unity, helps us in some small measure to understand it. In love the Father goes out of Himself and communicates Himself to the Son, in Whom is His delight and life. He imparts to the Son all He has and holds communion with Him in a life of giving and receiving. The Father has no life nor delight nor pleasure apart from the Son. That is the love wherewith Jesus loves His own. He gave Himself for them, imparts Himself to them, lives in them. He wishes to have no life apart from them. From the beginning of His love, in pitying them and sympathizing with them, He passed on to the love of good pleasure and fellowship, with a view to a unity in which they would dwell in Him, and He in them. His desire and rest was in them, and they learned *"to comprehend with all saints what is the breadth and length, and depth, and height; and to know the love of Christ, which passeth understanding"* (Ephesians 3:18–19). Only the Holy Spirit can lead the soul personally into that love. *"The love of God is shed abroad in our hearts by the Holy Ghost which is given unto us"* (Romans 5:5).

The love of God is such a supernatural, heavenly power that we might be tempted to make it merely a matter of thought, and by that means create some impression of it in our hearts. But a real participation in that love from heaven is such a divine matter that only those who have with great tenderness and wholeheartedness yielded themselves to be led and taught by the Holy Spirit can come to the knowledge of it. The love of God is plainly declared in Scripture to be the result of Christ dwelling in the heart. Only where the inner communion with the Lord has become in a measure the joy and experience of everyday can we know what the Lord meant when He said: *"continue ye in my love"* (John 15:9). *"Unto him that loved us, and washed us from our sins in his own blood, and hath made us kings and priests unto God and his Father"* (Revelation 1:5–6).

Let us consider Jesus as He was when, as man, He suffered and died for us, to give His blood for us. Let us allow Him to reveal in us the meaning and heavenly power of that blood. He will teach us that the most glorious fact in all His work is that it is the gift and bearer of His eternal, unceasing love toward us. Let us think of whither He is carrying us—it is to a full partnership in His kingly Priesthood and glory. He allows us to enjoy a foretaste of that love that makes us entirely one with Him and that will live forever in our hearts. Then our first and last thought about Jesus will be: Him who loved us.

4. TO HIM BE THE GLORY AND POWER FOR EVER AND EVER

The words of this song of praise are generally applied to God, but our Lord Jesus Christ is God, and they belong to Him also. He is worshipped here as our Redeemer. Now at the end of our series of meditations on His blood, and what He has obtained for us by that blood, these words of praise are a suitable expression for the feelings that ought to be ours—*"To him be glory and dominion [power] for ever and ever"* (1 Peter 5:11). These words came from a heart full of the joy of a personal experience of redemption. John writes as one who was living in the full enjoyment of the love of His Lord, who knew and felt in his heart that he was cleansed in the blood, and who experienced that Jesus had made him a king and a priest. His thanksgiving is that of one who rejoices with *"joy unspeakable and full of glory"* (1 Peter 1:8)—a joy kindled by the song of heaven to which he had been listening.

It is the glory and power of Jesus to bestow His love on a soul and to affect its cleansing in His own blood and to appoint such a one to His kingly priesthood. Then the heart overflows spontaneously *"To him be glory and dominion* [power] *for ever."*

Let us, as far as our knowledge goes, at every remembrance of His love, cry out, "To him be the glory." At times we are convicted that the praise we offer is too weak and too seldom heard, or that it has too little of the joy-note of heaven in it. But each conviction is a help to us if it drives us to seek after a fullness of Christ's presence within us that causes our hearts to overflow.

Yes, it is possible. Jesus lives and Jesus has loved us and has Himself cleansed us in His blood. He bestows upon us the disposition of kingship and priesthood by His indwelling.

It is possible. He can fill our lives with the experience that finds expression in the thanksgiving: *"To him be the glory and dominion* [power]."

My brethren, we hope to meet one day amid that multitude who have washed their robes in the blood of the Lamb and who never weary in singing: *"Thou art worthy...for thou...hast redeemed us to God by thy blood"* (Revelation 5:9). Let our exercises of preparation for that glory consist in the singing of that song: *"Unto him that loved us, and washed us from our sins in his own blood, and hath made us kings and priests unto God and his Father; to him be glory and dominion for ever and ever. Amen"* (Revelation 1:5–6).